# The Song of the Troubadour

## A Silent Eye Workbook

### Steve Tanham
**The Silent Eye School of Consciousness**

All Rights Reserved
Published by Silent Eye Press
The Song of the Troubadour, Revised edition
Originally published 2013
Copyright© Steve Tanham, 2013
Contributions by Sue Vincent & Stuart France
& The Silent Eye School of Consciousness
Edited by Sue Vincent
ISBN: 978-1-910478-03-5

Who wears the crown of thorns has might,
to build a kingdom and unite
Those lives below are his to guide,
but with his demons must he ride
Then will illusion drop away,
the heart will sing a different day
And glory will reveal its eye;
to love, to sing to live, to die.
*From the Song of the King*

# *Contents*

| | |
|---|---|
| Foreword | i |
| With Grateful Thanks | iv |
| The Story | vi |
| R1 – In From The Storm | 1 |
| R2 – A Confusion of Tongues | 16 |
| R3 – A Troubadour's Return | 34 |
| R4 – The Reluctant King | 48 |
| R5 – The Return of the Queen | 64 |
| Vigil and Dawn | 83 |
| The Opening of the Eye | 89 |
| *The Companions' Tales* | |
| The School | 123 |
| About the Author | 126 |

# Foreword
## *The Opening of the Eye - Accelerated Evolution*

Spiritual growth is a journey unique to each one of us, and taken whether we will or no. It is a natural evolution against which we may fight, actively resisting change or more usually with apathy and inertia. Or we may choose to jump into the flowing stream willingly, seeking the adventure of new destinations, unknown and unfamiliar landscapes seen in the light of increased understanding and awareness.

Some choose to walk their personal path alone, others choose the companionship along the way that a group, faith or school can provide. Within these are found many paths that lead towards a single, lambent Centre that is known by many names and yet transcends them all.

Each path will draw those to whom it speaks, as if both the path and the heart have a voice raised in song, and when the two come together in harmony, something beautiful is born. However, seeking that path that resonates with your own inner song can be a long and painful journey in itself, with many false starts and missed turnings.

One cannot teach spiritual growth. What can be taught, however, is a method, a pathway.

With the Silent Eye we seek to share a path into Consciousness that is an ancient one, not of our devising, but one that has lain hidden beneath an accretion of arcane symbols, correspondences and complex language. It is a natural and simple path, one that we have cleared of the accumulated debris of centuries, the brambles and thorns have been stripped away and it gleams clear and white before us as the newborn school opens its doors to students. We have, as Steve once wrote, given it a new life and a new language for the digital age.

To turn one's face towards this quest for understanding requires both commitment and awareness. There is no quick fix, no instant solution and no magic wand. Results are always dependent upon the dedication of the student. The destination is not reached overnight and the road may be long and rocky. But as with any journey, a well-constructed road, a map and clear direction makes it far more certain that the destination will be reached.

The active engagement in this journey has been called accelerated evolution, and that, I feel, is an apt description. The simple act of choosing to actively embrace the changing landscape of the path is, in itself, a powerful thing. The student who joins a Mystery School is guided by those who know the path ahead and can see the pitfalls before them having themselves walked the same way.

Seeds of knowledge are planted in mind and heart, for knowledge can be shared. Understanding grows with the student… and we are all students…and that unfolding is both personal and beautiful.

During the informal, and laughter-filled lectures that interspersed the ritual dramas of the launch weekend, the emotions thus awakened were combined with knowledge shared, simple and familiar concepts examined and explained in a new light, and understanding began to grow for all those present. I think this has been made clear by the articles the Companions shared with us after the event, some of which you will find at the back of this book.

In April 2013 the Silent Eye School of Consciousness was brought to birth with a very special weekend in the beautiful hills of Derbyshire. It was a weekend of dramatic ritual, a meeting of minds and hearts in love and laughter as members and friends of the School came together in what was, in my experience, a uniquely beautiful workshop.

The atmosphere was quite unlike any other I have attended, partly, perhaps, because it was the first for our new School, but undoubtedly it was mainly due to the people who had joined us to celebrate our birth. They came from across the world and from all spiritual backgrounds… shaman and magician, mystic and druid….some to join the School, others already core members… most simply to enjoy the weekend and lend us their support.

We shared laughter until we could laugh no more, we shared the deep and beautiful emotion of the work in temple, and a dawn high on a frosted hillside…and they moved me to tears on many occasions.

There were many who wished they could have joined us that weekend, others who do not know what to expect from a workshop of this nature…and it is for those that we decided to release the workbook. Steve Tanham's crafting of ritual drama deeply infused with the teaching we seek to share is as evocative as it is beautiful, capturing the essence of what we, as a School, seek to bring to life.

The annual weekend workshop in April is a central part of the School's year, open not only to students but to all, as are most Silent Eye events. The weekends consist of a series of fully scripted dramas around a single story, interspersed with guided journeys in consciousness and interactive lectures that generally end in laughter.

This book is a practical adaption from the original, designed to be read… or used…to gain insight into the inner workings of the personality and the enneagram as we use it within the School, and to give a glimpse inside a Mystery School at work. As well as the ritual drama you will find the accounts of some of those who were there for the birth of the School; subjective accounts that capture some of the magic and spirit of the weekend. I would like to thank their writers for their permission to include them in this book… and for being the midwives to the birth of a School.

In Loving Light,
Sue Vincent
*Director, the Silent Eye*
*2013*

## *With grateful thanks*

Many people have worked hard to bring the Silent Eye School of Consciousness to its birth, here in these beautiful Derbyshire hills. We would like to thank them all for their support and help. The past few months have been difficult but increasingly heartening; with the constant background thought that anything worthwhile takes a lot of effort.

The use of Ritual Drama is an ancient tool and a powerful one when it is carried out with love and integrity. It opens both the mind and the heart to new experiences, and those few hours, spread, in this case, over a spring weekend, linger in the emotional memory for many years to come.

That we chose to bring the Silent Eye to birth in this way is a testament to our magical past and those wonderful people who trained us in the ways of this arcane technique. It is our goal to make the Silent Eye School of Consciousness as modern as possible, but that does not mean it need lose contact with the ancient in the process. The dramatic psychological advances in Ego understanding now feature prominently in our approach, and we believe we have pioneered the mixture of "magical" teaching drama, combined with telling a single story over the course of a workshop.

Clarity of message will be our watchword. Whatever contributes to that will be used, within our capacity to understand it!

A few special thanks are due:

To the members of the former Eye of Horus SOL Lodge, many of whom decided to come with me on this journey into the partly unknown!

To Stella, Liz and the internal team at the Nightingale Centre. They have become great friends over the years

To the many who travelled to be with us on this special spring weekend.

And last but certainly not least, to my co-director of the Silent Eye, Sue Vincent, whose constant support and encouragement has got us this far, and to Stuart France, whose contribution has been deep and plentiful, and who has had to put up with the theatrical director's constant changes of plan!

In Love and Light
Steve Tanham
*Director of the Silent Eye School of Consciousness*
13th April, 2013

# *The Story...*

High on a mountainous pass, built into a wall of rock that separates two ancient kingdoms, lies the Sanctuary of Andasola. For centuries the home of a mysterious group of mystics, known as the Keepers of the Flame, this remote place offers a very purposeful refuge for those who come prepared. The Keepers have a very special skill – they can construct a set of psychological circumstances that produce rapid personal evolution for those with the courage to face the challenges that go with such an encounter. Masters of human nature, the Keepers welcome all within their stone walls, but treat nothing as coincidental. To arrive at the Sanctuary of Andasola is to be changed.

Two groups of people arrive at this high citadel on a dark and bleak night. The first are a group of Pilgrims – companions on a joint quest, whose very nature is emerging from the shadows of their own minds as they travel together. The second group comprises two Troubadours – holders of ancient lore which they convey in song, word and gesture to those who ask in the right way. With them is a child, a very special child – one entrusted to their care in this wild and dangerous landscape. The child has never developed its personality; it remains a pure Being, a vessel of light that can see the world as it is, rather than clouded with the accumulated dust of life's experiences.

But the Troubadours face a dilemma. They are on a mission to find and free a great King, a noble figure destined to rule a very special Kingdom; but the King is lost and believed to be a prisoner; and only the Troubadours possess the key to find him again. They have also sworn to look after the child. As they wrestle with these twin cares, their destiny brings them face to face with the Pilgrims in the Sanctuary, watched over by the Keepers, who see a very special purpose in the events unfolding before them, and that a great liberation is at stake that will demand their all.

With gentleness and love, the entire company comes to realise that they are all there for a purpose, that each has much to learn about their own lives through the encounter in the mountains.

# *In from the Storm*
## *Ritual Drama 1*

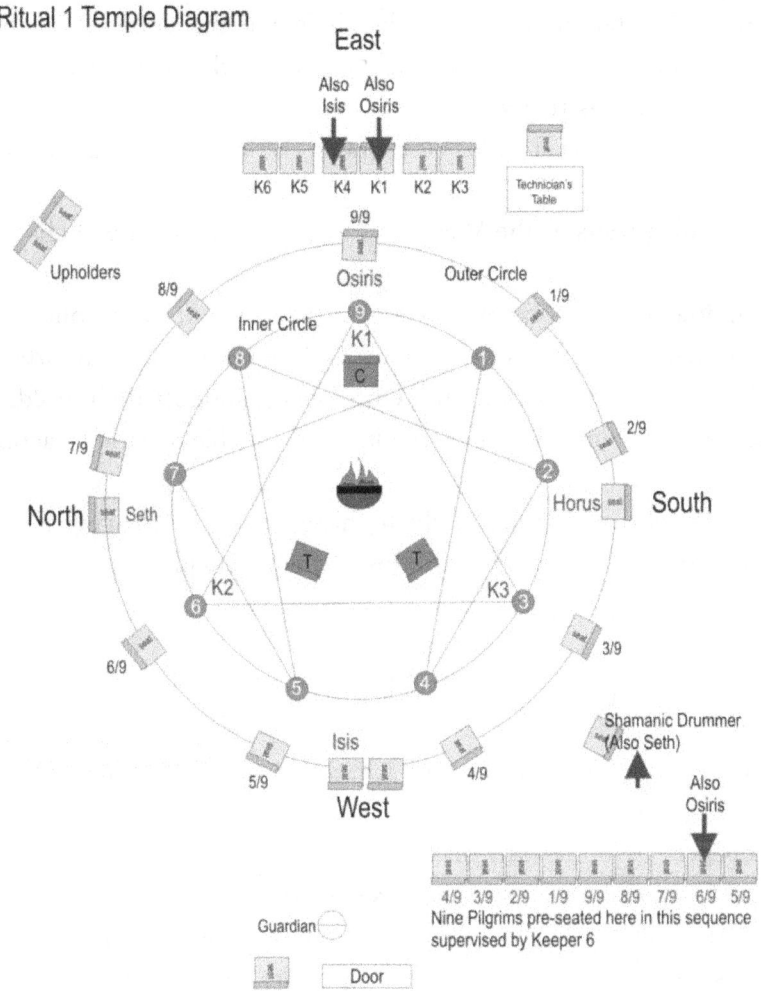

## *Temple Orientation*

The following diagrams are for Temple Orientation. They are provided for reference at this stage.

The Silent Eye temple combines the circle and the square. Movement in the temple begins with entry in the West and is usually clockwise, unless otherwise instructed.

The temple is intended to be very simple, with little decoration save a central flame.

The Guardian waits at the Western door. The Guardian will challenge you.

The Upholders group comprises anyone who is not doing one of the primary character parts in the dramas. Upholders are very important as they have the ability to view and, emotionally, support the unfoldment of the ritual without being involved in the inevitable tension of acting!

Where you sit depends upon which character you are playing. Beyond the Upholders, there are three groups of characters players:

1. The Nine Pilgrims.
2. The Six Keeper of the First Flame, who run the monastery of Andasola
3. The Two Troubadours and the Child they look after, marked as 'T' on the diagrams.

The Keepers sit in the seats marked 'K'

For the first ritual, they sit in the Keeper Row in the East. For all other rituals, they sit in the "compass" stations of East, South, West and North, shown here. The East is the opposite side of the room to the entrance, which is therefore the West.

The Nine Pilgrims sit around the outer circle until they are called into the enneagram figure, which is the inner circle. They always sit according to their numbers. For example, One of Nine (1/9) would sit next to position 1 of the enneagram.

For the opening ritual drama, they are in the inner triangle, but their normal position in the temple is in the West, in the outer circle, as shown. In this way they face whoever is in the East, the symbolic point of power in an esoteric temple.

This final diagram shows the full complement of Players.

## *Preparation*

Orange sashes for Gods, to be placed over shoulders when enacting, then taken off afterwards.
Additional chairs (6) in East for all Keepers.
Nine chairs laid out in the Outer circle, facing the enneagram circle numbers.
Nine electric candles are carried in the Child's bag.

## *Background to Ritual 1*

The nine pilgrims, travelling separately, have been cut off on the mountain pass by a severe storm and have found sanctuary in the Monastery of Andasola. The Keepers of the Monastery have welcomed them and given them food and shelter. They have been shown to their humble rooms where many of them have slept. Now, several hours later, and as though sleepwalking, they have been brought to the Temple.

For this ritual drama, four people are each playing two roles. The short opening sequence is hosted by the Gods: Osiris, Isis, Horus and Set. When the four players enact the Gods they place orange sashes around their necks, letting them hang down at the front, when they finish this short, introductory sequence, they return to where they were before it started.

After this, the scene shifts to the Monastery of Andasola, and the journey begins . . .

All Companions (except the Troubadours and the Child) are in the temple before the ritual begins. They enter in the sequence Keepers,

Nine Pilgrims, Upholders. The Troubadours and the Child remain outside. All bow to the Guardian and the Flame before taking their seats.

Apart from Keeper 6 who stays in the West to supervise the Nine Pilgrims, all the Keepers are in the Keeper Line in the East (see diagram).

The Pilgrims are seated in the temple before the ritual begins in a line along the West in the sequence below (this is supervised by Keeper 6, who returns to her seat in the Keeper line when the Nine are seated - see diagram):

Four of Nine. Three of Nine, Two of Nine, One of Nine, Nine of Nine, Eight of Nine, Seven of Nine, Six of Nine, Five of Nine.

# *The Ritual Begins*

*The Guardian ensures that the temple door is slightly open so that the Troubadours can listen for their cue. The Temple is not sealed at this point.*

*Technician plays Thunderstorm sound for 60 seconds.*
*After this, at the cue of Keeper 1 in the East, (also Osiris), the Gods, Osiris, Isis, Horus and Set put their orange sashes around their shoulders and come to stand in the temple quarters: Osiris in the East, Isis in the West, Horus in the South and Set in the North. They all face the central flame.*

**Osiris**
The storm gathers, First Children of the One. Below us the mind of mankind stirs into life. Once more, the light of understanding has its chance to shine.

**Isis**
We must send them love and fill them with courage, that their journey here is mirrored by an inner journey whose power is far greater. Pilgrims, indeed! If they but knew the extent of that journey!

**Horus**
But they must take those steps to Flight. We who watch must follow the High Laws of the Creator, the steps to the Crown can only be taken in Understanding, and that must always be fought for, though there is no foe

**Set**
But the Adversary is always present; the very product of incarnation, itself, and history says they will not master it, unlike the Pharaohs of old, whose lives depended on it!

**Osiris**
He does not reference the past as he casts the world anew into each moment. We shall see what steel lies in the hearts of they who now flee from the storm. Perhaps He will send Companions of the Resolution to help them?

*The Gods rise, bow to the flame, then re-take their former positions, moving clockwise around the inner circle to their seats (apart from Osiris/Keeper 1, who is already in the East), where they remove the sashes and place them under their seats. Keepers 1, 2 and 3 go, clockwise to enneagram positions One of Nine, Six of Nine and Three of Nine*

**Keeper 1**

Their journey here has been harsh, shall we let them sleep or call them forth.

**Keeper 2**

They have had a lifetime of Sleep

**Keeper 3**

Yes, let us bring them forth, for they will learn much by helping us in our Rites, they can carry on sleeping here in the temple!

*Keeper 1 goes to collect Four of Nine (4/9) via the outer circle, and takes them around the outer circle to their seat.*

*As soon as the previous Keeper has reached the Pilgrim, the next one sets off, taking each pilgrim to their seat from the line, in the sequence 3/9, 2/9, 1/9, 9/9, 8/9, 7/9, 6/9 and 5/9. In this way the three Keepers are in continuous movement, each taking a total of three Pilgrims of the Nine to their seats.*

*When all Pilgrims are seated in the Outer Circle, the Keepers return to the Keeper Line in the East. Keeper 1 remains standing. Keepers 2 and 3 are seated.*

**Keeper 2**

Let the Bells of the Monastery ring forth! The hour is late, but the call must be made.

*Technician plays the Monastery Bells for one minute*

**Keeper 1**

Now let the great magical unfoldment that is life, itself, be watched by those who are awake, and dreamed by those who are not!

*All sit in meditation for one minute.*

*Technician plays the Thunderstorm for one minute*

*The Troubadours and the Child wet their cloaks as from the storm, then enter the temple. They travel clockwise around the back of the outer circle. Then, they enter the inner circle through positions 1, 3 and 6, taking their cloaks off and shaking them as they take their seats as marked.*

*The Troubadours reach towards the fire on the central altar to warm themselves.*

**Troubadour 1**

Dear sister, what a night this is! And we still have so far to go. How will we reach the King in time, against such odds?

**Troubadour 2**

We will because we must, brother. There is no-one else that can save him.

**Troubadour 1**

Are we fools do you think? To set out to free a King whose whereabouts we know not!

**Troubadour 2**

Have THEY ever failed us, Brother?

**Troubadour 1**

No, they have not, Sister. You are right. The force of the storm outside has made me doubt my own resolve.

**Troubadour 2**

All you need is that resolve, Brother, and they will provide the rest. Have Faith! Greater forces are at work here than we can know ..

**Troubadour 1**

But we cannot travel with the Child. His sight is profound, but he is yet defenseless, and we need the speed of stealth in the darkness.

**Troubadour 2**

Then let us use our music to go inwards, dear Brother. And let it show us a way.

**Troubadour 1** picks up guitar and begins to strum.

**Troubadour 2** - Will you play our song? You know it fills me with a passion for what we do?

**Troubadour 1**

I will if you will sing it with me?

**Troubadour 2**

I will.

*Troubadour 2 comes to stand behind Troubadour 1, resting her hand on his shoulder.*

*Troubadour 1 tunes the guitar and begins to strum in preparation. As he does so, the Child rises and walks anti-clockwise around the circle, starting at 9/9 and gently touching the arms of each of the Nine Pilgrims until he comes back to his start-point at the end of the song.*
*Troubadour 1 stops strumming.*
**Troubadour 1**
He is very animated tonight! It is as though he sees something in these shadows?
**Troubadour 2** *studies the Child's movements*
I think he does see something in the darkness. You know his senses are acute and he can see what we cannot. His vision takes him into the very heart of things, and he feels their quality.

*Troubadour 1 begins singing (slowly), Troubadour 2 dances softly around him*

Let the song of the Troubadour bring you delight
That a flame may be kindled to burn clear and white
Let it tell of the road we have travelled so long
As we dance to tune of the Troubadours' song

*(Troubadour 2 comes back to his shoulder and joins in the song)*

For the song of the Troubadour marries the night
And gives birth to the Hawk of the morning in flight
As the Sun in its rising, heralds the day
And the Child in his silence, who shows us the way

For the heart of the Troubadour flies free and bright
On true wings of harmony, into the Light
We are guarded by shadows and live by the Word
That was whispered in silence and no man has heard

Let the song of the Troubadour gently invite
Come and share in the warmth of my hearthfire tonight

In the love-fuelled embers a vision may lie
That will speak in your
heart of your own Silent Eye.
*At the end of the song there is silence.*
*The Child has come to rest at position 9/9.*

**Troubadour 2** *(sadly)*
We did not set out to be so alone

**Troubadour 1**
Peace, dear Sister. We are not alone - now it is your resolve that falls away into the teeth of the storm!
*Troubadour 2 looks troubled but says nothing*

**Troubadour 1** *continues*
Whenever we have felt most alone, whenever the darkness threatened to consume us, we found there were other brave souls who would risk all and join us in our Quest. Have faith yourself!
*(He laughs and the dark spell is broken)*
Is my company so drab these days!
*(But Troubadour 2 does not answer, she has turned to look at the Child who has approached One of Nine and is gently pulling at ONE's arm)*

**One of Nine** *(shaking her head as though waking)*
I must have slept - the Keepers were so kind, and that meal so very welcome! My mind is full of visions. I feel so alive.
*CHILD switches on One of Nine's candle and gives it to her, then pulls her to position One of the enneagram, where they remain standing. One of Nine looks startled as she suddenly sees both the Child and the Troubadours.*

**Troubadour 2** *(pointing)*
Brother! Look what he has done!
*Both troubadours gaze in wonder at One of Nine, who is staring at them.*

**Troubadour 1**
Dear Pilgrim from the shadows. Do not be frightened; what you see is real, but in the world of outer darkness, invisible. Trust your new eyes. The Child has brought you to us. Stay with us if you can!

**One of Nine** *(hesitantly)*
I, I . . will try. I have often dreamed that one could travel to places of

other-reality like this. Who are you?

**Troubadour 2**

We two are Troubadours, communicators of an ancient way. *(laughs softly)* We are not angels, just mortals as yourself who have set our lives on a course to bring the Light of Understanding into the world, with love and gentleness but never force. The Child is a special being whose qualities you may get to know. Will you stay with us for a while. We have need of companionship on this dark night?

**One of Nine** *(recovering her composure)*

I will. I feel a great inner warmth in this place and that storm would drive anyone insane! But I have business beyond this place and it is important.

*Child continues clockwise around the circle to light the candle of Two of Nine, who he pulls to her feet and into her place in the enneagram, giving her the candle.*

**Troubadour 2**

Brother! He grows in Being faster than we could have hoped! I think he means to wake all these souls who sleep!

**Troubadour 2**

Yes, Sister. We dare not disturb this process!

**Two of Nine**

What is this place? I am sleeping in my bed, finally safe from that foul storm, I know I am. How can this chamber be so vivid and real?

*Two of Nine stares at the Troubadours, seeing them for the first time.*

**Two of Nine** *(looks at the Troubadours)*

Who are you? and who is she?

*(Two of Nine looks at the standing One of Nine)*

**Troubadour 1**

All will be explained when the Child's work is finished, dear Friend. Do not be alarmed. You are in a safe and peaceful place.

*Child continues clockwise around the outer circle to take the hand of Three of Nine.*

**Three of Nine**

What is this place? The Keepers fed us so well, but then I slept, I think. And now I have awakened in this strange chamber!

*Child pulls Three of Nine to her feet, gives her a lighted candle and takes her to*

*Position Three.*
**Three of Nine** *(looking at the Troubadours seeing them for the first time.)*
Who are you? *(Three of Nine looks around at the others standing)* and who are they?
**Troubadour 2**
All will be explained in a few moments, dear Pilgrim. Do not be frightened. You are in a safe and peaceful place.
*Child continues clockwise around the outer circle to take the hand of Four of Nine.*
**Four of Nine**
What is this chamber? That meal was so welcome after the cold of the storm, but I must have eaten too much and fallen asleep. Now where am I?
*Child pulls Four of Nine to her feet, gives her a lighted candle and takes her to Position Four. Four of Nine stares at the Troubadours, seeing them for the first time.*
**Four of Nine** *(looking at the Troubadours)*
Who are you? and who are they? *(Four of Nine looks around )*
**Troubadour 1**
Please do not be frightened. You are in a safe and peaceful place. You are here because your SOUL permitted it. All will soon be explained.
*Child continues clockwise around the outer circle to take the hand of Five of Nine.*
**Five of Nine**
Where am I? I was praying in my room after that life-saving meal! But this chamber is very different!
*Child pulls Five of Nine to her feet, gives her a lighted candle, and takes her to Position Five on the enneagram. Five of Nine stares at the Troubadours, seeing them for the first time.*
**Five of Nine** *(looking at the Troubadours)*
Who are you? *(Five of Nine looks around at the others standing)* and who are they?
**Troubadour 2**
Pilgrim, you need have no fear. You are in a safe and peaceful place. You are here because you were called from the Shadows. All will become clear, soon.

*Child continues clockwise around the outer circle to take the hand of Six of Nine.*
**Six of Nine**
Where am I? I was reading in my cell, now suddenly I am in this chamber!
*Child pulls Six of Nine to his feet, gives him a lighted candle and takes him to Position Six. Six of Nine stares at the Troubadours, seeing them for the first time.*
**Six of Nine** *(looking at the Troubadours)*
Who are you? *(looks around at the others)* and who are they?
**Troubadour 1**
Please, have no fear. You are in a place of Sanctuary. On some level of your Being, you wanted to be here. All will soon be explained.
*Child continues clockwise around the outer circle to take the hand of Seven of Nine.*
**Seven of Nine**
Where am I? I was studying my books, now suddenly I am in this chamber! *Child pulls Seven of Nine to his feet, gives her a lighted candle and takes her to Position Seven. Seven of Nine sees the Troubadours for the first time.*
**Seven of Nine**
Who are you? *(Seven of Nine looks around)* and who are they?
**Troubadour 2**
You need not be frightened. This is a safe place and you have been welcomed by those whose who look after weary pilgrims on the path. This place will become more familiar, soon.
*Child continues clockwise around the outer circle to take the hand of Eight of Nine.*
**Eight of Nine**
Where am I? After that wholesome meal, I was stroking my fur coat and drifting into a deep sleep, now, suddenly, I am in this chamber!
*Child pulls Eight of Nine to her feet, gives her a lighted candle and takes her to Position Eight. Eight of Nine stares at the Troubadours, seeing them for the first time.*
**Eight of Nine**
Who are you? *(Eight of Nine looks around)* and who are they?
**Troubadour 1**
You need not be frightened. This is a safe place and you have been welcomed by the Keepers of the First Flame. You are safe from the

wildness outside.
**Eight of Nine**
Hah! The Wildness outside seemed tame compared to what is going on here!
**Troubadour 2**
Peace, sister Pilgrim. Let the stones of this sacred place work its gentle magic!
*Child continues clockwise around the outer circle to take the hand of Nine of Nine.*
**Nine of Nine**
By the Gods, where am I? After that fine meal, I was slumbering deeply, now, suddenly, I am in this chamber full of strangers!
*Child pulls Nine of Nine to his feet, lights his candle and takes him to Position Nine. Nine of Nine stares at the Troubadours, seeing them for the first time.*
**Nine of Nine**
Who are you strangely garbed pair? You remind me of minstrels from my past? *(Nine of Nine looks around at the others who are standing)* And who are they?
**Troubadour 1**
You need not be frightened. This is a safe place and you have been welcomed here by the Keepers who have made this place a Sanctuary since ancient times. All are welcome from the storm.
*The Keepers all Stand*
**Keeper 1**
Pilgrims, companions, be welcome here. Troubadours, once more we throw open our hospitality and warmth to you brave souls. It may be that you being here is no accident - that your lives meet here at a strange nexus, where none would have dared predict it.
**Keeper 2**
Please do not fear this. It is the sort of experience that we may have only once in our lives.
*(clasps his hands over his heart).*
Open yourselves to it, and see what is written into the books of your lives over the short period you are with us as our guests.
**Keeper 3**

Cherish it . . . For a few short hours, you may find yourselves plucked from the Storm of life and graced with a new set of Eyes.

**Keeper 4**

My Brother speaks the truth. You have been lifted from the worlds of shadow, where everything appears permanent but nothing truly is. This place is the world of inner meaning, where, for a short time, you may write in a book that is seldom open to you. Here you may act in a way that is closed in the shadow-world. Seize it while you can!

**Keeper 5**

And do not fear us or our strange ways. For ages past we have looked after the interests of those on the narrow Pilgrims' Path that led you up from the lowlands to the High Country beyond this range.

**Keeper 6**

If you will but relax into it, you will find sustenance here, of a higher order than you have known before.

*Child begins to move clockwise, again. Stopping at Position One, he steps onto the beginning of the Enneagram figure and looks at Troubadour 1, smiling.*

**Troubadour 1**

Very well, precious and precocious Child of Light. You may walk the Soul of the Circle, but then you must leave the chamber for now. You, too, need rest.

*Technician plays music while the Child walks, slowly:*

*Child walks the sequence 1-4-2-8-5-7 and back to 1. Then he bows, laughs, and dances out of the chamber following the outer circle clockwise.*

*Technician fades out the music, if it is still playing.*

**Troubadour 2**

Companions, fellow travellers on a sacred path, you can see that we have guarded and nurtured the Child. But our strength is limited, and we have another task to perform, which is of great importance. Will some of you accept responsibility for his wellbeing for a while?

*Looks around the circle and as she does so, the* **Companions** *begin to respond, slowly at first, then more loudly, they all say, individually "I will".*

**Troubadour 1**

This gladdens our hearts. You can see that this is no ordinary child, and our Gathering will be brightened by his presence, if we can keep him safe, and nurture his young awareness of our world.

**Troubadour 2**
Companions, be warm and extend your friendship to each other. Draw the Fellowship together with your goodwill, for tomorrow will tax us all. We, too, must rest, for, beyond your tasks with the Child, we have far to go when the Sun rises again.

*Technician plays Track 4 Monastery Chanting*

*Troubadour 1 and Troubadour 2 bow to the flame, then move to the outer circle, leaving clockwise.*

*When they have done so, all Companions leave in the sequence, Keepers, Nine Pilgrims, Upholders.*

*Candles are given to the Guardian on departure and switched off.*

*Guardian closes the temple.*

## *End Ritual 1*

# *A Confusion of Tongues*
## *Ritual Drama 2*

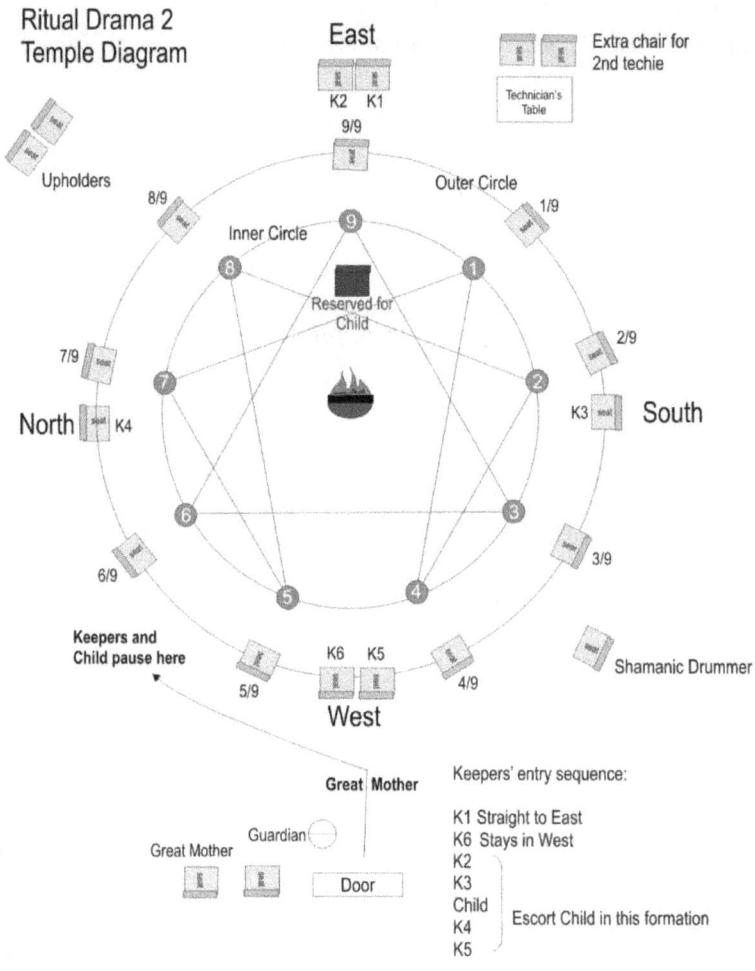

## *Preparation*

Extra chair for second technician.
Chair for Shamanic Drummer in South West.
Opening positions:
The technicians are pre-seated in the temple.
The Great Mother and the Guardian are already in the temple, standing in the West as shown.
The Companions, the Keepers and the Child are outside the temple.
Guardian and Technicians are already inside the temple.
Guardian opens the door to the Temple.
Technician
Technician plays the sound of the Monastery bells, loud enough for all to hear beyond the doors.
Guardian
The Guardian challenges each. When satisfied, they are allowed into the temple.
All initial movements are made around the Outer Circle, and behind the chairs.
When those entering have passed the Guardian, they pass to the Great Mother, who blesses the journey each is about to take. After this, they make a gesture of Love and Respect to the Flame and pass into the temple.

## *Sequence of entry:*

Technician plays music for the entrance of the Nine and Upholders, stopping it when all the Nine have entered and taken their seats.
Upholders enter next. They take their seats the North East.
Technician Plays Monastery Chanting for the duration of the entry of the Keepers.
The Keepers then enter, in the sequence:
Keeper 1, Keeper 6, Keeper 2, Child, Keeper 3, Keeper 4 and Keeper 5.

Keeper 1 walks, clockwise to the East station using the outer circle.
Keeper 6 walks straight to the West quarter.
Both stand facing the flame.
Keeper 2, Keeper 3, the Child, Keeper 4 and Keeper 5 stop in the North-West and form a line with the Child between Keeper 2 and Keeper 3, as shown. They wait until Keeper 1 calls them forward.
Technician
Technician plays Thunderstorm 4, softly, while the Keeper 1 speaks, then fades it down as the Guardian seals the temple.

# The Ritual Begins

*The Nine enter first. They pass the Guardian and the Great Mother*
*When those entering have passed the Guardian, they pass to the Great Mother, who blesses the journey each is about to take, embracing each in turn.*
*After this, they make a gesture of Love and Respect to the Flame and pass into the temple.*

**Keeper 1** *(from the East)*
Guardian! Please close and seal this sacred temple of the Mysteries.
**Guardian** *(performs the temple sealing)*
It is done, Keeper of the First Flame.
*Guardian and Great Mother are seated.*
**Keeper 1**
Then let us begin. Will those bearing the Child bring him to the East and thenceforth to the Flame.
*(In the line formation shown, the Child is escorted to face the East)*
**Keeper 1**
Beloved Child. We welcome you back into this sacred chamber. Those guarding you will now escort you to your seat by the Flame. We hope you will add your light to its glory.
-*The Escorting Keepers stay in formation and escort the child clockwise from the East towards the West,*
*Keeper 3 only travels as far as the South and stops at the quarter.*
-*Keepers 2, 3, 4 and 5 continue with the Child to the West.*
-*Keeper 4 stops in the West (joining Keeper 6).*
-*Once in the West Keeper 2 takes the Child to the flame (see below) and Keeper 5 continues on around the circle to the station in the North.*
-*From the West, Keeper 2 takes the Child to the flame, where they both bow, then on to his seat on the Eastern side of the flame.*
*The Child is seated.*
*Keeper 2 passes directly to the East to join Keeper 1.*
*(Guardian sits)*

**Keeper 1**

Companions, you are gathered to provide care for the Child, and we will guide you in that caring. You find yourselves in a strange place high in these mountains, but you are safe here. Let us renew the spirit of your Quest and open this temple with love in our hearts, for there is much to accomplish before the Troubadours return.

Before we formally open the Gates of the Temple, let us take advantage of an act of good fortune. Late last night another traveller arrived, a shamanic drummer, a man of few belongings, but immense skill and depth. We took him in with our customary hospitality, and he has asked if he might repay that by censing our temple with his sacred drumming. No repayment is necessary, for we live to serve the Light, but we are happy to accept his kindly offer, and feel it will enhance the temple. Will the Shamanic Drummer please come to the East to perform this rite.

*Drummer comes from the West, to the East, bows to Keeper 1, and begins the drum censing, moving in the sequence East, South, West and North on the inner circle. When finished, he bows to the East and returns, clockwise, via the outer circle, to his seat in the West.*

**Keeper 1**

Thank you, Drummer. I feel that the sacred sounds you have created for us here have raised the spiritual level of this temple.

**Keeper 1** *(Raises her hands, palms outwards to face the flame)*

I open the gate of the East, with the word La *(stretched out into a chanted Laaaaaah)*. This sound signifies and is linked with, the forces that brought into existence the starry Galaxy, the Milky Way which is the founding energy for our very lives. In the Ray of Creation, La is the third note in the fundamental octave which brought us into Being.

**Keeper 6** *(from the West)*

Companions, from time immemorial, temples of the mysteries have been laid out in a sacred shape to convey a message to the deepest part of the mind of each of those taking place. Before you here are two circles and a symbolic flame.

The outer circle represents the outer circle of humanity and also the world in which we live, formed from our reactions to life. The inner circle represents the state of the awakened Seeker, whose attitude to life changes in line with his or her resolve to turn Seeking into Finding.

The flame in the centre of the temple represents the Essence of each of us. It is our own measure of Being or Spirit - that gift of our uniqueness from the Cosmos, which we brought into this life and which has been added to, via the container of the Soul, by the life lived. Between the two is an ancient figure, a sacred seal from the distant past, whose purpose is to show us that there is a tide and a sequence to all things in the physical and non-physical world; and that this is related to everything unfolding in our lives.

*Pauses*

The Personality is a thing of this lifetime and will not survive transition. It therefore dies with the body, to be returned to whence it came. Only the memory of the life lived will remain with the Soul, and that will live forever. But something else remains after so-called death, the Understanding and Wisdom that we have truly made our own becomes added to the Soul's Essence and stays with what is truly us forever.

Soul must be understood, for there are many different things said about it. The Soul is the Substance of the Consciousness. It lives at whatever level it is allowed to, but that is under the control of our ordinary minds.

When the consciousness of a person is made whole, the Soul becomes a living and vertical channel of consciousness at all levels of their being at the same time, seeing inwardly and outwardly in a continuous, single act of vision and realisation. The Soul knows its own nature well, but it does not yet know the World fully. It is the role of the conscious mind, and the ordinary Ego, to explore, experience and determine its own limitations. Although this happens to few of us, when it is accomplished, the Ego becomes the fuel for the journey Home.

The Soul or Essence is therefore a vital part of life, if we are to find a meaningful, individual life that surpasses the limitations of the body and the death of the personality. The Child is the perfect emblem of this Essence and we must now symbolically bring it into this life, and let it experience the world with all its love and rawness. If we carry this out well and with integrity, the Child's personal evolution will be greatly enhanced.

I open the gate of the West with the ancient sound of "Fa" *(draw out into FFaaaaaaaaaaaaaaah)*, symbolic of the Planetary level of the sevenfold Ray of Creation and the fifth note in the descending octave that brings the Universe into being. A sequence of Creation which comes to its fruition, for us, with the genesis of the Earth and Moon.

*All Keepers now stand.*

**Keeper 1**

Will the Nine now join us, taking their places on the numbers of the enneagram.

*(The Nine go to their allotted places on the enneagram and stand facing the flame in the centre of the temple.)*

**Keeper 1**

I now call upon you all to introduce yourselves to this company. Take time to be your Selves in this holy place. Here there is no judgement, no guile. All who pass through these ancient walls share the same journey. Nine of Nine, will you tell us who you are?

*Keeper 1 is seated (all Keepers should now be seated, and speak from their chairs)*

**Nine of Nine**

My story is a sad one, but I will tell it as best I can.

*(pauses and takes a deep breath, drawing himself taller)*

I was once the King of a land far from here. The years and the wanderings have dulled my mind, and, to be honest, I could not tell you, now, which way it lies.

*(Pauses)*

My father's Kingdom endured a savage and war-torn period, and my coming into this world was amidst this time of constant war and strife. My mother was killed shortly after I was born, though I have some memories of her. I was raised to be a fighter by my father, the old King, although I hated that life. Dutifully, I followed my father's wishes and became a warrior, and, indeed there were many battles that bore the signature of my skills with the blade. But my heart was elsewhere, as though the distant touch of my long-dead mother still pervaded my life, with its warmth and gentleness.

When my father died, mercifully in his own bed, the crown passed to me. This gave me some freedom for the first time in my life and I took the chance to bestow peace on our lands, encouraging the use of trading treaties with our neighbours and the general pursuit of barter and commerce to replace the blood-feuds of old.

**Keeper 2**

So your actions did you credit. Why then are you a King in exile?

**Nine of Nine**

My fall from grace was a very public one. My actions brought ruin on the kingdom. A wily King from a neighbouring land saw my attempts at a sustained peace as a sign of weakness, and began to raise an army against us, while, at the same time, allowing my Son to marry his daughter. When the attack came, we were taken by surprise, and the Kingdom was overrun. My life was spared but I became a puppet and my subjects rose up against me and had me banished.

**Keeper 2**

But you are a noble victim of such times, nevertheless?

**Nine of Nine**

Yes, but what use is that now? *(raises his head and snorts at the sky)*

I live a half-life, wandering here and there, spending time with whoever among my blood-relations will still speak to me. I suspect that the only reason I was left to live was to increase the suffering and the humiliation! I would be better off dead!

**Keeper 3**

How do you know you are alive?

**Nine of Nine** *(glares back)*

You would add to my humiliation?

**Keeper 3**

No, once great King. Our ways here are direct, but my words carried no malice. My provocation was not to your conscious mind.

**Nine of Nine**

Hah! Games, games! I have had enough of others' games. I live now for a peaceful life, away from the grinding wheel of the world, *(smiles and looks fondly at Three of Nine for whom he has an attraction, she smiles back)* with a warm bed and good food. My subjects are far away but I still wish them well. After what they endured under the Butcher, I could not blame them for my exile.

**Keeper 4**

Then let us leave you in your exile for a moment.

**Six of Nine**

I, too, know what it is like to be haunted by the past. I have great sympathy for this King.

**Three of Nine**

And I too. *(smiles and laughs)* and your bed need not be cold here, dear King, and I am sure my legendary dancing will warm your spirits, too!

**Nine of Nine** *(looking delighted at this support)*

My new friends, this is kind of you, but I feel the Keepers mean no harm!

**Keeper 4**

We do not. But we speak directly to those who have ears to hear; and this room has floors that cannot be seen.

**Three of Nine**

Riddles dear King. Riddles, are you not tired of a life of riddles!

**Nine of Nine** *(cautiously, as though sensing that hidden things are taking place)*

In my ordinary way, yes, lovely Dancer of the Ages, but did we all come here merely to continue the lives that we led before?

**Three of Nine** *(smiles coquettishly)*

Very well. But remember my offers . . .

*Nine of Nine smiles and nods, but says nothing.*

**Keeper 5**

But our flow of introductions was interrupted. Let those in the circle take their turns, for the shape has its meaning and contains great purpose within its geometry. *(points to One of Nine)* Good lady, will you tell us something of yourself and your journey here?

**One of Nine**

I hesitate to do so, for I find myself next to a King, and you may not believe me when I say that I am of royal blood, in fact I am a Queen. A Queen travelling incognito and in search of a great secret.

**Keeper 5**

We would not pry where our questions are unwanted, but can you tell us more?

**One of Nine**

Many years ago, a great Alchemist passed through our land. He taught many things to those who would listen, but I was younger and missed much of the inner meaning of his words. The men at court were fools and lusted only after the Gold he said he could make from the most base of metals! Even I could see he mocked them!

Soon after that he left us, silently and in the middle of the night. But his words lingered in my mind, and many times have I made pilgrimages to find his trail. I am impatient to test my understanding and find the missing key.

**Keeper 5**

Must they be spoken by him?

**One of Nine** *(looks shocked at the thought)*

But they were his words, how could another speak them? *(becomes angry)* Do you speak in riddles, too?

**Keeper 5**

Within these hallowed walls, we find that the truth is shared by many, as though another had placed the words in all our mouths. Perhaps you could tell us what questions impel your travels so?

**One of Nine**

*(Angrily)* Perhaps I could! *(then, softening, as she realises how she has reacted and draws a breath)*

The Alchemist spoke of a journey, one that could be taken within a man or woman as a boatman might take a mighty river back to its source. The men-fools had no time for this, but I sat at my father's knee and listened hard. I could see in my mind how this would happen . . . but now that I have the time and the freedom, I know not where this river begins! *(holds up and clenches her fists then smiles at her own anger)*.

And, as you can see, I am not a patient Queen!

**Keeper 6**

There may be others here, who know of such a way?

**Seven of Nine**

My rank is far below yours, gracious Queen, I am a mere Chancellor of another realm, yet I too search for answers and would gladly assist you in this. My role in the royal court makes use of much precision. I would put my powers of thought and computation at your service.

**One of Nine**

That is a gracious offer, sir. But I have little need of assistance. As a woman in a time dominated by men, I am my own way!

**Seven of Nine** *(bows)*

As you wish, but my life has taught me that a little planning can save a thousand steps in the wrong direction!

**One of Nine**

And your offer was gracious and kindly taken, but I make my own way in the world.

**Keeper 6**

And you, Lord Chancellor. In what direction would your thousand steps take you?

**Seven of Nine** *(laughs)*

My, but you people are direct for dwellers in holy places! You are unlike any I have met before!

**Keeper 6**

We are a poor Order, my lord. But our biggest lack is time; and so we speak directly.

**Seven of Nine**

Time?

Surely here in this mountain fastness, trapped by snow for most of the year, you have all the time you could wish for?

**Keeper 6**

I did not speak of our time . . .

*Seven of Nine nods thoughtfully and smiles, but says nothing further.*

**Keeper 1** *(smiling, good naturedly)*

Our attempt to use the circle to greet each other is fraught with challenges today! Let us return to its boundary in our greetings! *(looks at Two of Nine)*

**Two of Nine** *(draws herself tall, and draws a deep breath, preparing to be imposing)*

I am a Physician. My story is simple: I am here because I seek the Truth, but in my own unique way. My methods are known across many lands, and I am the author of numerous books. My medical knowledge has been used in the service of both peasant and royalty *(looks around)*, I may even have treated the families of many of those present. I am the leading authority on the treatment of disorders of the blood.

**Keeper 1**

And what do we or the Troubadours have to teach one of such eminence?

**Two of Nine**

I cannot speak for the others, but I am here simply to gain access to the high land that borders this one. Sanctuary from that foul storm outside is my only wish, and I am grateful enough for that. *(pauses)* Beyond that, if my unique medical skills are of use to any, then I will gladly contribute. As to the absent Troubadours, I do not pretend to understand what drives them on such a strange and demanding quest; but I wish them well.

**Keeper 1**

And what do you hope to find in the high land beyond Andasola?

**Two of Nine**

Why, the answer to a long-forgotten question!

**Keeper 1**

May we ask?

**Two of Nine**

You may, but I will not share it. It belongs to my heart alone.

**Four of Nine**

Then may your heart know joy, sir.

*Two of Nine looks with disdain at Four of Nine, who shrinks into herself.*

**Keeper 1** *(watching the exchange)*

Very well. We will not press you, physician. Be welcome and sheltered here.

*Two of Nine nods to Keeper 1 in acknowledgement and says nothing further.*

**Keeper 2** *(looking at Four of Nine)*

And you sir, you bring intensity and some gaiety into this dark chamber. May we know your story?

**Four of Nine**

My story is a much humbler one than those around me! How I wish my life were like theirs! I am a poor player - a simple actor who earns his crust from performing in the travelling theatres. I wander and perform wherever I can earn my living. Sometimes I sing and tell stories - whatever I can do at the time, amidst all the fine lives of others.

I am a simple man; and I am honoured and a little cowed in this company. Please forgive my bright and battered clothes - they are the tools of my trade and I need to travel light!

**Keeper 2**

We make no outer distinctions here, poor player. We look at different garments. All are welcome under this roof. What fortune has brought you so far into the frozen wilderness and so ill-prepared for this ordeal?

**Four of Nine**

My years of playing and touring have created a mind that feels it is always dreaming! I have heard that there are those in these parts that can restore clarity to such a man as I?

**Keeper 2**

And where do you seek such guidance?

**Four of Nine**

I seek it wherever it may be found.

**Keeper 2**

Then from the mouth of a humble man comes wisdom. Be welcome here, player. Let no man or woman claim to be your superior under this roof.

**Four of Nine** *looks around furtively then bows to Keeper 2*

Thank you - I mean no offence to anyone.

**Keeper 3**

And none will be taken.

**Keeper 3** *(looks at Five of Nine)*

And you, fine lady. What brings one so richly dressed into this encounter?

**Five of Nine**

My story is also a simple one. I have riches and can afford to travel. I also seek only sanctuary here. I am on my way to the high land beyond Andasola to find new merchants with whom to trade my gold and jewels. The encounter with the Troubadours moved me, and I will gladly lend my talents to looking after the Child for these few days, but beyond that, my interests lie with my riches and how to increase them - in that I am also a simple person.

**Keeper 3**

Does nothing here speak to different rooms in the house of your Soul?

**Five of Nine**

I know nothing of any Soul. My life is happily contained and controlled within my intellect. From its high windows, I can survey the world and the path to further riches that lies ahead of me. In that pursuit lies sanity, for we live in a cruel world and one must provide for oneself, for no-one else will!

**Keeper 3**

And are you not being provided for now, here in this high sanctuary?

**Five of Nine**

Well, yes. And I am grateful, but that will not distract me from my purpose here.

**Keeper 3**

Then we will see if we cannot add to your riches in other ways!

*(Five of Nine looks slightly confused at the notion that there could be "other ways", but says nothing)*

**Eight of Nine** *(looking at Five of Nine)*

My sympathies are with you, Merchant of fine jewels. I also hold out nothing of hope that anything here will change me. Life is a simple process where one must conquer to eat, where we dominate or be dominated. I would rather decide on what to feast than have another feed on me! I love my life and control it as ruthlessly as fortune permits! I also only seek passage through here. I want and need nothing more. The rest I can take.

**Keeper 4**

We welcome all here, but what is your living, that brings you so far away from the kind of cities in which you must be so much more at home?

**Eight of Nine**

I run a circus - the biggest circus in all these parts. I am known throughout the lowlands. I specialise in training wild animals, *(laughs)* bending them to my will. I am here only because some have said that a rare wild cat lives high above this snowline, and I hunger for a new pet!

**Keeper 4**

There are many animals in these parts. Take care, bold lady, lest their bite exceeds your passion!

**Eight of Nine**

None has so far, priest. *(Keeper 4 smiles and bows to Eight of Nine)*

**Keeper 4**

Then safe passage to your land of wildness!

**Eight of Nine**

Those around me need safety! I fear nothing!

**Keeper 5** *(looking at Six of Nine)*

But I think that your character is of a less brash nature, traveller?

**Six of Nine**

Yes, very much so. I am really a fugitive here. I was wrongly accused of theft while travelling and have been pursued to your border. Please do not betray me!

**Keeper 5**

We have said that all are welcome here - saint or sinner, both are welcome in this place of last refuge. You need not fear any authority here, save your own Soul.

**Six of Nine**

Well, I would wish that my soul were strong enough to protect me, like

the circus lady over there!
*(looks across at* **Eight of Nine** *who mutters "weak fool" as she shoots back a withering gaze).*
**Six of Eight** *(nods, accepting the scorn)*
But, as you can see, I am not made that way. The only strength I know is running away from danger and having the intelligence to avoid trouble.
**Keeper 5**
But you will sleep safely here.
**Six of Eight**
I do not sleep easily.
**Keeper 5**
None of us would sleep easily if we knew how closely our deaths marched behind us. But we persist in living as though Life will last forever! Let us not waste what little time we have . . .
**Six of Eight**
I am so very grateful for what you have done for me. I will help with the Child in any way I can.
**Keeper 5**
Thank you.
**Keeper 6**
And now that we have been introduced, and have seen what a diverse group of souls the storm has thrown up on these icy wastes, let us ask the Child if he would like to say anything to those who would be his guardians?
**Child** *(stands and goes to face One of Nine)*
I see you clearly. You are clever like the Troubadours, but you seem so very Angry. You could help me, but your anger will drive us apart.
**Child** *(goes to face Two of Nine)*
I see you clearly. You are skilled in the pathways of life, but you are full of Pride. You could help me, but you would shun me with your glittering presence.
**Child** *(goes to face Three of Nine)*
I see you clearly. You are full of brightness and fun, but there is

something deeper that should be there. A light is missing in your eyes, beyond your gleeful presence and your shining words. You could help me, but you face the wrong way.

**Child** *(goes to face Four of Nine)*

I see you clearly. You are a simple man, but your heart is heavy and you see yourself as small. You could help me but I need those who are sure in their footsteps and whose hearts are not full of envy.

**Child** *(goes to face Five of Nine)*

I see you clearly. Your head is large. You live in a Tower in your mind. You could help me but your eyes are blinkered and only open to what lies before your hands. You would collect me!

**Child** *(goes to face Six of Nine)*

I see you clearly. I feel the fear that is your life. You could help me, but what I need would frighten you.

**Child** *(goes to face Seven of Nine)*

I see you clearly. I can taste the hunger in you for more and more. To me you want to eat the world. You could help me, but what I am would be just another meal on your table.

**Child** *(goes to face Eight of Nine)*

I see you clearly, and you frighten me. *(Eight of Nine feigns mock horror).* You snarl at the world and glorify the animal that you worship inside. You could help with your bravery but you would turn me into another pet. *(Eight of Nine smiles at him and nods).*

**Child** *(goes to face Nine of Nine)*

And you could help me most of all. Your courage and sight are great. You are wounded within from a thousand battles but your heart is stout and unbowed.

*(pauses and places his right hand on the King's heart)*

But you are asleep to what you should do. The care of others has drowned your Soul.

*Child walks back to the flames by his seat to warm his hands.*

**Keeper 1**

Companions in the Hall of the Flames. From the mouth of the Child comes great wisdom. Let those with ears to hear, do so.

And now it is time to retire and take refreshments. Let us consider what we have learned about each other, and ponder where these pieces might fit together!

Guardian! Unseal the temple that we may rejoin the mundane world and its life.

*Guardian unseals the temple*

**Keeper 1**

Let us take our leave and meet again later. I do not need to tell you that there is a great purpose in this room, and the Troubadours will add to that on their return. Try to open your hearts to the needs of others, and thereby see the needs in your own souls.

*The Child goes to stand in the West and is escorted out of the temple by the Officer there.*

*The Nine leave in a clockwise circle, led by Four of Nine who goes straight to the exit via the West gate.*

*The Keepers leave, entering the greater circle and moving clockwise until they get to the West.*

*All bow to the Flames and then to the Great Mother and Guardian as they pass out of the temple.*

*The technicians, Great mother and Guardian are the last to leave.*

## *End Ritual 2*

# A Troubadours Return
## Ritual Drama 3

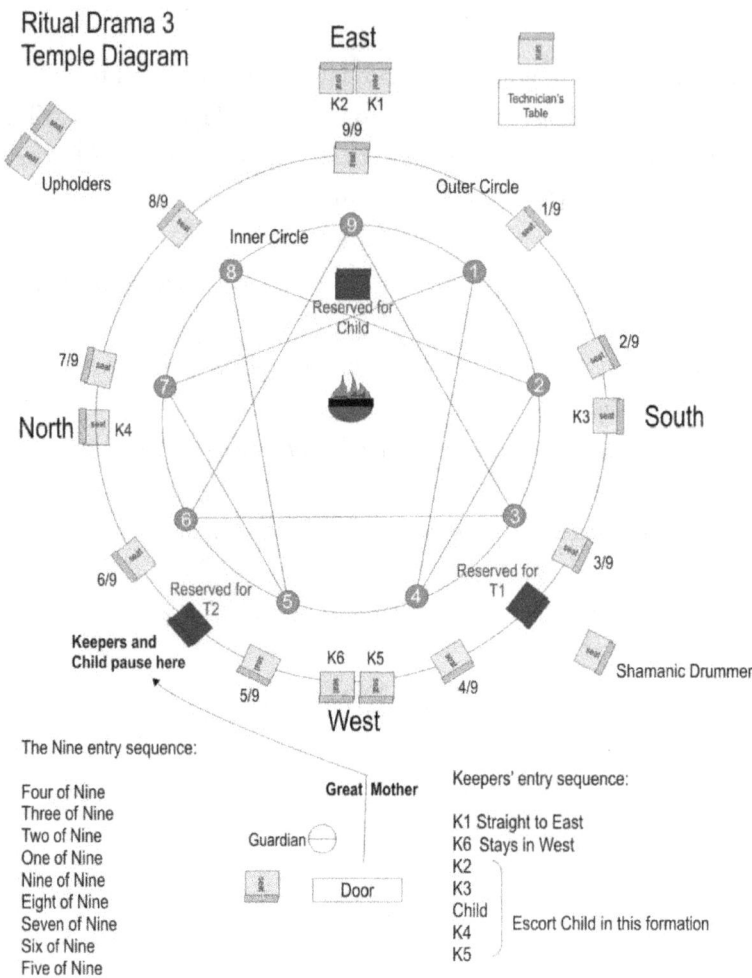

### *The Song of the King*

In troubled land, by him begotten, he calls to those who have forgotten
On crystal tower and legend's stage his voice is lost in honest rage
It passes those who fear and face, and dances from their joint embrace,
In courtly wealth and gilded pride, no song within their toughened hide
In lusty life or perfect death the royal song brings on the deaf
Until it reaches Kingly ears, asleep and turned for twenty years
Who wears the crown of thorns has might, to build a kingdom and unite
Those lives below are his to guide, but with his demons must he ride
Then will illusion drop away, the heart will sing a different day
And glory will reveal its eye; to love, to sing to live, to die

# *The Ritual Begins*

*The Guardian and Technician are inside the temple*
*Technician plays the sound of the Monastery bells, loud enough for all to hear beyond the doors.*
*At the end of the bell ringing,*
**Guardian** *says:*
You may enter the Temple
*Technician plays music for the entrance of the Nine, stopping it when all the Nine have entered and taken their seats.*
*The Guardian challenges each companion. When satisfied, they are allowed into the temple.*
*The Nine enter first. They pass the Guardian and take their seats as shown in the diagram in the Outer ring.*
*Other Companions, who are not of the Nine or the Keepers enter next. They take their seats at any of the non-reserved places in the North East.*
*Technician Plays Monastery Chanting for the duration of the entry of the Keepers.*
*The Keepers then enter, in the sequence:*

*Keeper 1, Keeper 6, Keeper 2, Child, Keeper 3, Keeper 4 and Keeper 5. Silent Eye April 2013 The Song of the Troubadour ©International Copyright Silent Eye School of Consciousness, 2013 Page 58*

*Keeper 1 walks, clockwise to the East station using the outer circle.*
*Keeper 6 walks straight to the West quarter.*
*Both stand facing the flame.*
*Keeper 2, Keeper 3, the Child, Keeper 4 and Keeper 5 stop in the North-West and form a line with the Child between Keeper 2 and Keeper 3, as shown. They wait until Keeper 1 calls them forward.*
*Technician plays a few seconds of Thunderstorm 4.*

**Keeper 1** *(from the East)*
Guardian! The storm rages outside, but we have the power to shut it out of this sacred place, and thereby come to know our inner truths. Please close and seal this sacred temple of the Mysteries.

**Guardian** *(performs the temple sealing)*
It is done, Keeper of the First Flame.
*Guardian is seated.*

**Keeper 1**
Then let us begin. Will those bearing the Child bring him to the East and thenceforth to the Flame.
*(In the formation shown, the Child is escorted to face the East)*

**Keeper 1**
Beloved Child. We welcome you back into this sacred chamber. Those guarding you will now escort you to your seat by the Flame. We hope you will add your light to its glory.

*-The Escorting Keepers stay in formation and escort the child clockwise from the East towards the West, -Keeper 3 only travels as far as the South and stops at the quarter.*
*-Keepers 2, 3, 4 and 5 continue with the Child to the West.*
*-Keeper 4 stops in the West (joining Keeper 6).*
*-Once in the West Keeper 2, takes the Child to the flame (see below) and Keeper 5 continues on around the circle to the station in the North.*
*-From the West, Keeper 2 takes the Child to the flame, where they both bow, then*

*on to his seat on the Eastern side of the flame. The Child is seated.*
*Keeper 2 passes directly to the East to join Keeper 1.*
*(Guardian sits)*

**Keeper 1**

Companions, you are familiar with the rite we perform here. We will not repeat its purpose.

Will the Shamanic Drummer please come to the East to cense this temple with sound.

*Drummer comes from the West, to the East, bows to Keeper 1, and begins the drum censing, moving in the sequence East, South, West and North on the inner circle. When finished, he bows to the East and returns, clockwise, via the outer circle, to his seat in the West.*

**Keeper 1**

Thank you, Drummer. I feel that the sacred sounds you have created for us here have raised the spiritual level of this temple.

**Keeper 1**

Our time here is short. Let us be on with the sacred duties we must perform while the storm still rages.

**Keeper 6**

Companions, I have had word that the Troubadours will shortly return. They will need our spiritual support and comfort, for the scout says their faces are graven. Let us prepare the Temple to receive them in love and companionship.

**Keeper 1** *(Raises her hands, palms outwards to face the flame)*

I open the gate of the East, with the word La *(stretched out into a chanted Laaaaaah).*

**Keeper 3** *(Raises her hands, palms outwards to face the flame)*

I open the gate of the South, with the word Sol *(stretched out into a chanted Soooooll).*

**Keeper 6** *(from the West raises her hands, palms outwards to face the flame)*

I open the gate of the West with the ancient sound of "Fa" *(draw out into FFaaaaaaaaaaaaaaaah).*

**Keeper 4** *(Raises her hands, palms outwards to face the flame)*

I open the gate of the North, with the word Me *(stretched out into a*

*chanted "may").*
*All are seated apart from the Keeper of the East (Keeper 1)*

**Keeper 1**

Fellow Keepers of the first flame, thank you for your assistance. Our sacred temple is now closed to the mundane, but opened to the inner love and intelligence that we seek. Let each of us watch our thoughts and feelings so that our presence here is adjusted to its purpose. Will the Nine now join us, taking their places on the numbers of the enneagram.

*(The Nine go to their allotted places and sit facing the flame in the centre of the temple.)*

**Keeper 1**

Companions of the Nine, you undertook to join us in looking after the Child, Are you all prepared to affirm that you are still true to this quest? Please speak for yourselves in this, and if any are in doubt, let them leave us, for we approach a critical time in our work!

**One of Nine** *(stands)*

The Child is wonderful, but I could do so much more with him - think of how he could be educated within my royal world! *(pauses)* But I know that is not in your gift. I will work with you while we await the storm's passing. *(Sits)*

**Two of Nine** *(stands)*

The child looks healthy and bright and I can see no way in which my advanced skills might be of use to him, but I will gladly offer what services I can. *(sits)*

**Three of Nine** *(stands)*

The Child is lovely. I would love to take him home with me! I would dress him in the finest clothes and show him off. He would love life with me and my friends would adore him! *(Sits)*

**Four of Nine** *(stands)*

The Child reminds me of all that I have lost. I long to follow him and play and watch how he views the world. How wonderful it would be to be him! I will gladly help you in whatever way I can *(Sits)*

**Five of Nine** *(stands)*

All children are fine, but they have little to do with the needs of running our busy lives. They are better looked after by others - with us keeping a watching eye on them, of course! I can see nothing that I can add to this gathering, but if I am of value keeping my distant eye on things then that is fine with me. *(Sits)*

**Six of Nine** *(stands)*
The way the child runs and skips reminds me of my former carefree days. But now it hurts me to see one so free! But his little soul warms my heart and I will gladly search for strength within myself to help him in any way you wish. *(Sits)*

**Seven of Nine** *(stands)*
This child has little to do with my life. My former wife looked after our children and left me to do the important things in life, such as becoming rich! Children require far too much time and care, and should be left to those who relish such things.

**Eight of Nine** *(stands)*
The Child is feisty and not afraid. I would love to drink in his vitality and train him to work with animals as I do. He would be a great addition to our troupe. But you may not have that in mind . . . so I will happily work with you, but don't expect me not to watch him closely by day and night as I would with any exotic and wild thing! *(Sits)*

**Nine of Nine**
Your hospitality is great and we are in your debt. I will gladly add my heart to caring for this child, though he strikes a sad chord in me that takes me far back to my own childhood days. It seems so long ago that such innocence was in my life!

**Keeper 1**
Then I thank you all and, although not all of you are filled with joy at the prospect of looking after him, you all seem content to be a part of it. Now let... *(is interrupted by a single loud knock on the temple door)*
*The Guardian interrupts, striking his staff, loudly, twice.*

**Guardian**
Keeper of the Flame. The Troubadours have returned. May I admit them into this sealed and sacred chamber?

**Keeper 1**

You may, Guardian. They will be tired from their long journey. Let us hope they bring good news!

*Guardian strikes his staff three times.*

*Guardian opens the temple door and the two Troubadours enter, bow to the Guardian and move directly to stand at their seats, Troubadour 2, clockwise to the North West, Troubadour 1 to the South West (directly, i.e. anti-clockwise)*

**Keeper 1**

Greetings, Troubadours! we are in awe of your efforts to find and free the fabled King. Has your long journey brought you success?

**Troubadour 2**

Alas, Keeper of the Flame, we bring sad news. We sought the advice of the hermit in these hills. He studied the parchment then directed us to a castle in the mountains. But we arrived to find it in ruins, sacked by wandering hoards from the North some months ago, and now unoccupied. We did not find our King.

**Keeper 6**

Why this is sad, indeed. But you are known for your discernment. Does the parchment contain so much of a riddle?

**Troubadour 1**

We have skills, dear Keeper, which you have helped us hone in the past, but they are not sufficient in this case.

**Keeper 1**

The Pilgrims are assembled as you see. The Child is here. All is well. Let not despair enter this quest. Read the parchment one more time and let us see if we can, together, shed some light on this puzzle.

**Two of Nine**

My skills are well known. My intellect is legendary! Let me hear your words and I am sure I will penetrate to their real meaning!

**Seven of Nine** *(yawns)*

Oh must we? Can we not pass these necessary hours in doing something that will be of value?

**Keeper 1**

Companions - be patient! You are not here by accident. Learn to look

within to the jewels that True Life places, glittering, in your path, as its divine humour urges you on! Come Troubadour, read us the parchment one more time.
**Troubadour 1**
The Song of the King…

In troubled land, by him begotten, he calls to those who have forgotten
On crystal tower and legend's stage his voice is lost in honest rage.
It passes those who fear and face, and dances from their joint embrace,
In courtly wealth and gilded pride, no song within their toughened hide
In lusty life or perfect death the royal song brings on the deaf
Until it reaches Kingly ears, asleep and turned for twenty years.
**Troubadour 2** *(takes over the reading)*
Who wears the crown of thorns has might, to build a kingdom and unite
Those lives below are his to guide, but with his demons must he ride
Then will illusion drop away, the heart will sing a different day
And glory will reveal its eye; to love, to sing to live, to die.
**Keeper 5** *(to the Troubadours)*
And what did you take as the overall meaning of this?
**One of Nine** *(interrupts)*
It is obvious what it means! One who has been forgotten seeks to join again with those who search for him. The start-point of the Troubadours' search for the ransomed King, surely?
**Four of Nine**
But this speaks of more than that. I see in this a great tragedy. It hints at a story within a story.
**Two of Nine**
That may be so, but its words are plain. As the royal lady here says, this is the start of the search and one who is lost means to be found. This rising song speaks to the Troubadours alone, but like all poetry, it meanders along.
**Eight of Nine**
There are many ways to be found, we can find ourselves in pleasure

and wildness as much as in duty! But I am uneasy at some of the references here. To me it smacks of hidden meaning!

**Five of Nine**

We will know nothing if we do not consider the whole. It is foolish to make assumptions without that high perspective - then we can judge whether there is any meaning in it at all! In my experience few things are worth the involvement; it is better to watch and wait, the happiest outcome is to decide, in the light of logic, not to become involved.

**Seven of Nine**

I see no return on this speculative thought. Let us be on with our tasks!

**One of Nine**

But the verse is well-written. There may be deeper and perfect meaning here, if we have the will to find it.

**Child** *(stands and looks round at the Nine)*

Are you so blind that you cannot see what is in front of your eyes and ears? This is no chase in the mountains, this is about your very Selves!

**Four of Nine**

You can be a precocious child!

**Troubadour 2**

No! Let him speak. This is a child in one sense only. His being is developed in a way that we, all, are not. He may be immature in the ways of the world, but he carries truth and wisdom within him.

**Troubadour 1**

We accompany the child, and have done so for many months. If you consider his words as though hearing a new kind of voice for the first time, you will learn much.

*(looks at the King and Queen)*

Even you, your Royal Highnesses, will gain from this.

**Nine of Nine**

Hah! For many years I listened, Troubadour. And look where it got me - I am a King without a Kingdom. But I have given my word and I will listen to the Child if that is what you and the Keepers wish.

**One of Nine**

You share this chamber with those of great intelligence, Troubadour.

Be careful not to arouse their wrath!
**Troubadour 1**
Your Highness. I have spent many years in prisons for arousing wrath. My fear has been burned from me; from us, for my sister has shared that fate, too. Do not seek to threaten us, for we bring only a quest for Light into this Sanctuary.
**Keeper 1**
And let no-one threaten others here! This is a house of peace and nurture, and all are equal under its roof. Those not in tune with this sentiment may take their chances with the storm!
**Queen** *(looking angry but perturbed)*
I mean no offense, Keeper. But something strange works within these walls and I feel uncertain of my ground - uncertain of what it is doing to all of us!
**Keeper 2**
Sometimes, uncertainty is the only thing that will open us to that which is truly new - to that which is alive.
**Nine of Nine**
But some of us may be finished with the new, Keeper.
**Keeper 3**
But is the new finished with you, my Lord?
**Troubadour 2**
Child, seize the moment and do not fear. Speak as you had begun to.
**Child** *(looking around hesitantly)*
I will . . I see fear all the time in those around me, hidden sometimes in what is said, but there still. Fear and Indolence and Deceit. I can only speak of what I see.
**Troubadour 1**
Please go on and tell us what your eye reads in these lines.
**Child**
I see a Song, rising to be heard. A calling to those who have the ears to hear.
**Keeper 4**
And to whom does this song call, Child?

**Child**
It calls to all in this circle
*(sweeps his arm around the circle)*
**Keeper 6**
All of them equally?
**Child**
Yes, and that is what it says. It tells of something deeper than they are all aware of. It points to why they do not hear it - it points to why they are here!
**Four of Nine**
It points to why we are here? The Song of the King links us together in something? But I thought it was simply for the Troubadours?
**Child**
They did, too! But their role was to bring it into this chamber. To face defeat of purpose so they could look on new purpose from its ruins. . .
**Two of Nine**
This is stretching the laws of belief! Surely you don't think that we are all here for the same purpose, rather than sheltering from the storm, on our way to our own goals in the High Land beyond this Kingdom?
**Troubadour 1**
I have learned to trust in great purpose, Physician. Now my eyes begin to open to what the child is saying. Please let him continue.
**Child**
Let me show you how the song works. It comes from a higher realm. It does not walk time in the way we do. It sees patterns differently. It belongs to this Shape of Seven in the middle of the temple, though it has not yet revealed its inner workings. *Child moves to stand on enneagram point 1*
**Child**
You did not see, but as you questioned what the Keepers said, your words walked like this:*(Child walks through the enneagram via points 1-4-2-8-5-7- and back to 1)*
**Three of Nine**
But you called it a "shape of seven", but you only counted out six

moves as you walked, then you began again with the first?
**Child**
Yes - the shape is an eternal recurrence. It describes how the hidden causes bring things into our lives and how that is the reality and not what we see.
**Child**
Here, let me take you all on its journey; then you can stop thinking about things and begin to feel them more. *Child takes each of the Nine around their own Shape of Six, beginning with One of Nine and missing out Three of Nine, Six of Nine and Nine of Nine.*
**Three of Nine**
But you missed out three of us!
**Child**
Yes, the shape is part of three designs in one glyph. There is an outer circle which represents the passing of Ordinary Time. Within that there is the Shape of Six, or Seven if you see its deeper meaning, which represents an inner way of seeing and doing; which connects events in a way not normally seen by people. The Shape of Six is placed next to a different shape - the Shape of Three, which describes a higher purpose, one whose control rests here with the King and his two subjects - the Fugitive and the Dancer. Here, let me bring you to your real King.
*Child goes to Three of Nine (Dancer) and takes her up the line to Nine of Nine, the King, who begins to look very uncomfortable. Then he walks back along the same line to Point 3 and across to Point 6, collecting Six of Nine (Fugitive) and taking him to Nine of Nine (King). At this, Nine of Nine is looking very agitated.*
**Nine of Nine** *(in anguished tones)*
No, No - I do not want this! *Six of Nine and Three of Nine take the King's hands to steady him.*
**Six of Nine**
King of former greatness, have faith. We, too, do not understand what happens here, but can you not feel the beating of great and invisible wings in this room?
Is this sense of awe, this presence not what we Pilgrims have searched for? Have faith with us! Trust it!

**Three of Nine**

Yes! And we will walk this wonderful design with you. I have seen enough of your true character to know that I would gladly serve you, whatever happens.

**Nine of Nine**

But that is all in my past. I made a ruin of one Kingdom, do not ask me to condemn another. Keepers! *(holds his head up in anguish and shouts)* - free me from this, I do not want it!

**Troubadour 2**

But listen to the words:

"Until it reaches Kingly ears, asleep and turned for twenty years"

Yes, great King, the parchment spoke of this and not of any search out there in the mountains. We are truly blessed by something of great import. The Child has shown us the way. You are turned away from your destiny, you have the chance to return to it!

**Troubadour 1**

Yes, my Lord, she speaks the truth, listen to the words again:

"Who wears the crown of thorns has might, to build a kingdom and unite those lives below are his to guide, but with his demons must he ride"

*King shakes his head in refusal, then hangs his head down and is silent.*

**Child**

There. The pattern has been walked. The King, though unhappy, is re-united with his most trusted Servants! I do not understand people! *(putting his hand innocently on the King's heart and speaking softly to him)* This is what your heart most wants!

**King** *(sobbing quietly as he speaks)*

You are kindly, Child, but you know nothing of ruin.

**Three of Six** *(speaking softly to Keeper 1)*

We are linked with the King in a special way?

**Keeper 1**

Yes, you two are, and that is well perceived.

Your role is to support the King as he learns to exercise his will in this sacred chamber to achieve a very special destiny. The Child sees this pattern but cannot find the words of the world to describe it. The King wrestles with his past, his Demons, but as with him, we must all one day face that which we have buried. How that battle goes determines how we walk forward into the true Light of our real Being.

**Troubadours** *(together)*
Have faith great King. The beating wings call to you.

**Three of Nine and Six of Nine** *(softly)*
Have faith dear friend. We will be with you.

**Keeper 1**
Have faith, once noble servant of the Flame. Many is the pot that thought itself smashed beyond repair. You may be surprised at what your mighty Soul can yet hold.

**Keeper 4**
The hour is late, and there is much emotion in this chamber. Let us retire and take refreshment. We will return to this chamber and this moment when we next gather here. We have much to resolve and even more to change. Guardian - Open the gate of this Temple.

**Guardian**
Yes Keeper. *(Taps staff once, and opens the door. Then when West door is open)* The Sacred Chamber is unsealed.

*The Troubadours follow their semi-circles to the East to join the King, Dancer and Fugitive. The five of them stay in place. (The Child leaves with the Keepers)*

*The Child goes to stand in the West and is escorted out of the temple by the Officer there. The Nine leave in a clockwise circle, led by Four of Nine who goes straight to the exit via the West gate.*

*The Keepers leave, entering the Outer circle and moving clockwise until they get to the West.*

*At the door all bow to the Flames and then pass out of the temple, bowing to the Guardian. The five in the East stay until the rest have gone, then they leave quietly.*

# *End Ritual 3*

# The Reluctant King
## Ritual Drama 4

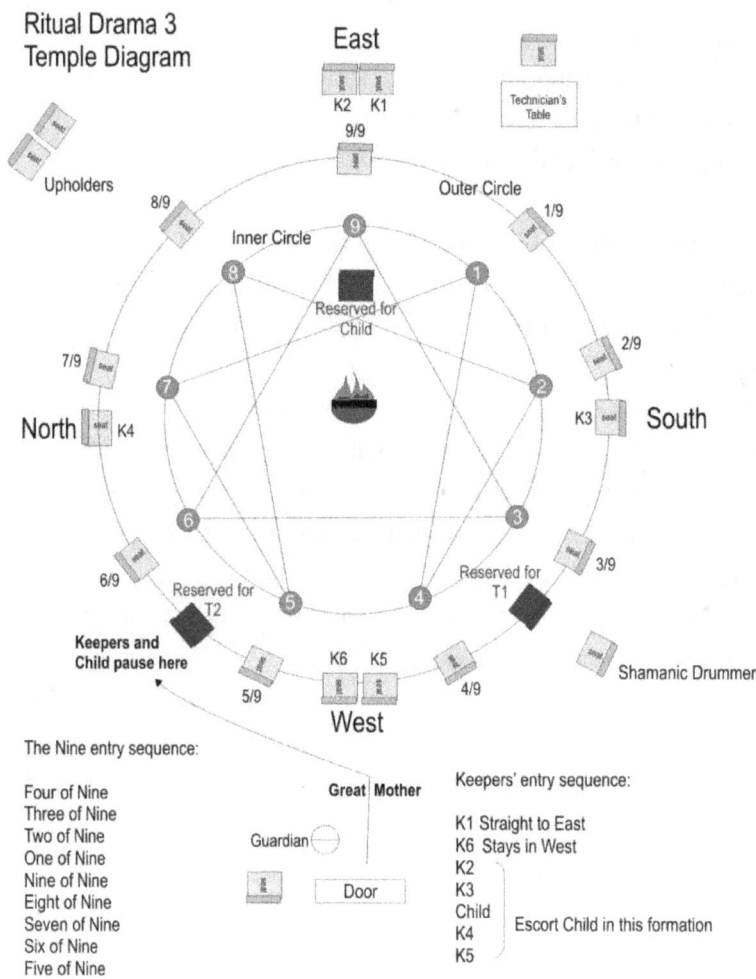

Ritual Drama 3
Temple Diagram

The Nine entry sequence:

Four of Nine
Three of Nine
Two of Nine
One of Nine
Nine of Nine
Eight of Nine
Seven of Nine
Six of Nine
Five of Nine

Keepers' entry sequence:

K1 Straight to East
K6 Stays in West
K2
K3
Child
K4   Escort Child in this formation
K5

## The Song of the King

In troubled land, by him begotten, he calls to those who have forgotten
On crystal tower and legend's stage his voice is lost in honest rage
It passes those who fear and face, and dances from their joint embrace,
In courtly wealth and gilded pride, no song within their toughened hide
In lusty life or perfect death the royal song brings on the deaf
Until it reaches Kingly ears, asleep and turned for twenty years
Who wears the crown of thorns has might, to build a kingdom and unite
Those lives below are his to guide, but with his demons must he ride
Then will illusion drop away, the heart will sing a different day
And glory will reveal its eye; to love, to sing to live, to die.

# The Ritual Begins

*All companions resume their places as at the end of R3. All are seated.*
*Technician plays the sound of the Thunderstorm for one minute*

**Keeper 1** *(stands)*
Guardian, seal the temple and let us resume our work.
*Guardian seals temple then says*
**Guardian**
Keeper of the First Flame, this sacred place is tiled, once again. The profane is separated and the Will of the One is with us.
**Keeper 1**
Thank you, Guardian. Now let us return to the work with the Child and the plight of the King, who seems to resist that which is placed before him.
**Nine of Nine**
I do not resist it. It is destined for another. I merely acknowledge that.
**Keeper 2**

Do you think that we will not help you in this?
**Nine of Nine**
I do not think anything
**Keeper 3**
Do you live in fear of this?
**Nine of Nine**
How can I live in fear of something I do not acknowledge?
**Keeper 4**
But not to acknowledge is not the same as not knowing.
**Keeper 1**
Troubadours, it is time for you to exercise your art at a deeper level in this.
**Troubadour 1**
Dear King, once as proud and as mighty as any. Let us send you someone who understands Fear even more than you do . . .
**Troubadour 2** *(speaking to Six of Nine)*
Lowly fugitive, now safe within these walls. You truly have nothing. You claim no land as your own. Your life consists of your mind, your heart and the breath in your body. Will you risk even that to help the one we claim as your King?
**Six of Nine**
I will.
**Troubadour 1**
Then go to him now, for he needs to see this from one who has suffered even more than he has.
**Troubadour 1** *(continues, looking now at Three of Six)*
Vibrant dancer. We see beyond your glitter. We see a wounded soul who knows what it is like to be rejected. We see the inner curves of your exotic dances that speak of the sadness that lies at the heart of your soul and makes you seek the adoration that the famed dances bring you. Will you make yourself complete by going to the King and offering yourself to him, that in his hour of greatest need he may count on your faith and love?
**Three of Six**

I will, Troubadour.

Though I do not know what impels me to do this in this strange chamber, but I do know that I have never felt such power and purpose within my life before. If the price of this wellspring of real vitality is to risk my reputation defending the Wounded King, then that is a gift I will gladly bestow.

**Troubadour 2**

Your resolution sets an example for us all. But go now to the King who does not want you but needs you so very much.

*Six of Nine and Three of Nine go up their sides of the triangle directly to face the King. They hold out their right hands to him.*

**Nine of Nine** *(shaking with emotion, speaks softly)*

Dear Friends, I know you little, yet what you do in this strange room touches me so very deeply. Would you both really sacrifice all you have and are to be with me in an uncertain future?

**Three of Nine and Six of Nine together**

We would.

**Nine of Nine** *(softly)*

Then let me take your hands and have you come and stand by me as we gaze out into this strange land now before us. I have no idea what to do next but I do sense that something vital is being born in this temple.

*(King touches their hands and they stand to his left (dancer) and right (fugitive). They leave a moment's silence, then says:*

Now return to your stations and be vigilant for me. This shape before us on the temple floor is full of power, and I have seen such power used for both good and ill.

*Three of Nine and Six of Nine go back along the inner lines of the triangle to their stations, where they remain standing.*

**Keeper 5** *(to Nine of Nine)*

Now you must do what all do whose eyes have been opened: you must look at the world through them as though you had never seen it before.

**Nine of Nine**

But how do I do that? I long to be able to see with new eyes, but my past haunts my thoughts and my emotions.

**Keeper 6**

As with all of us, dear companion. And now we must show you, and those brave souls who have agreed to accompany you, how to see with new eyes.

*Three of Nine and Six of Nine are seated.*

**Keeper 1**

Child, will you take this once-great man on another journey around this temple. Will you show him the shape of his world and the motives of those whose lives surround him?

**Child** *(nods and faces Nine of Nine)*

They think they move in the world - your world, but they are asleep to what they are, and you must see where they came from to understand how to free them all!

**Nine of Nine**

Free them all?

**Child**

Yes, for that is a task that only a King may perform. But now you are not alone. You have she who dances for the adoration of the world, yet sacrifices that for you; and he who is the very heart of fear, yet fears no more because of you. They are both at your side as you discover who is really in this chamber.

**Nine of Nine**

Show me Child, for my mind swims and is dizzy with the import of this!

*Child takes the King and moves around the circle to stand facing One of Nine.*

**Child** *(quotes)*

"In lusty life or perfect death the royal song brings on the deaf"

One half of that line is for this Queen, icy in her wintery perfection, but cold. The perfect death, indeed!

**One of Nine** *(rises)*

I will have none of this! I know who I am and what I came here to do.

**Child**

Do you? Do you really know who you are?

To me you are a woman who lives an angry life, searching for a perfection she will never find, because she does not know that her life is governed by that search and not by its goal!

**One of Nine** *(falteringly as though wounded by the truth)*

What. . what . . how dare you!

**Troubadour 1**

It is too late for the defences of habit, Queen of Anger and Perfection. Now you must know that your role here is to be a Queen to the King, and to share in his rulership, and that, behind this anger lies a greater and more beautiful set of qualities.

*(One of Nine glares silently back at the Troubadour and is seated as the King moves away)*

*(Child takes Nine of Nine along the internal line to position 4 to face Four of Nine)*

**Nine of Nine** *(as they are walking)*

Troubadours, why do we walk this way and not along the natural line of the circle? What is it about this internal shape of recurrence that so determines these moves?

**Troubadour 2**

You may not believe me, King, but I will say it anyway. The shape is one of the signatures of the Great Creator of the World and derives from the sacred properties of the circle or rather the sphere, itself. When you walk this path, you are walking with God, and sharing in the movements of what the church calls the Holy Ghost.

*Child takes the King to stand before Four of Nine.*

**Child** *(quotes)*

"On crystal tower and legend's stage his voice is lost in honest rage"

See now before you the figure who is legend's stage. This fine actor, known for his performances of great tragedies, masks another man - one whose life is full of envy. Whoever he sees and values makes him wish to be them. He cannot live for himself for he is full of the envy of others. Can you bring such a one into your new Kingdom?

**Four of Nine** *(rises)*

I am hurt by this. I am a gentle soul and wish no-one harm.
**Child**
There are many forms of harm, but perhaps the greatest is to hide behind the untruths that we construct for ourselves.
**Four of Nine** *(falteringly as though wounded)*
I will confess to Melancholy. But I strive to give all of myself when I make my performances.
**Nine of Nine**
If I am to assemble a new royal court, one that functions in this different world opening up before us all, then I will need such a one as you. But we must each of us know the difference between the truth and the acted. For that quality, I will seek your undertaking.
**Four of Nine**
Then I look to you, my King, to show me these virtues that are needed in your new court. *Nine of Nine places his right hand on the left shoulder of Four of Nine and smiles.* All will be well if we can work in honesty and truth.
*(Four of Nine is seated as the King moves away) Child takes the King to stand before Two of Nine.*
**Child** *(quotes)*
"In courtly wealth and gilded pride, no song within their toughened hide"
Here is your Gilded Pride - a skilled man, but one so full of his own importance that he is closed to the real life that flows around him!
**Two of Nine** *(rises)*
Take your tricks elsewhere, child. I will have no part in this! There is nothing that I need to learn from those in this room!
**Troubadour 2**
Physician, do not insult the Child with the word "tricks" - that is the very thing that he cannot do. There are many things that you might learn from his honesty and from the others in this chamber.
**Two of Nine**
I have spent my life learning. Am I not renowned for it?

What would I learn from a Child such as this, honest though he may be?
**Nine of Nine**
You wear the Shell of the Seeker. What did you come to find, Pilgrim?
**Two of Nine** *(looking less sure of himself)*
Well, that is another matter, and a goal of a different nature. But you and those in this room could only offer me knowledge, and the shell covers the harvest of my lifetime, which is full of that.
**Troubadour 1**
And what do you value beyond Knowledge, Pilgrim? What Alchemy of life's knowledge would be held behind that Shell, should it ever fulfil its purpose?
**Two of Nine** *(sensing his logical danger, and getting angry)*
I want to KNOW beyond KNOWING damn you, Troubadour. I want to have so much knowledge that it bursts its walls and lets me UNDERSTAND *(then more softly, realising what he has done)* Surely I have deserved that?
**Child**
Such knowing lies not in more knowledge, dear and glorious scholar. It lies in the eternal Being of the Moment.
**Nine of Nine** *(nodding his head and looking with great sympathy at Two of Nine, then putting his right hand on the Physician's left shoulder)*
It does dear Friend. The Child speaks the truth. For me, to be the mightiest and most dutiful warrior of his age was not enough, though that was forced upon me.
For you the world's knowledge is not enough, for it has not been kissed with the eternal Grace of Being. Stay with us Pilgrim, and I will try to show you the truth of these words.
*Two of Nine hangs his head, nodding slightly, but refusing to fully acknowledge it.*
*Two of Nine sits.*
*Child takes the King to stand before Eight of Nine (who rises)*
**Child** *(quotes)*
"In lusty life or perfect death the royal song brings on the deaf"

One half of that line is for this ring-mistress of lusty life, so very capable of taming the outward life and bending it to her whims, but so helpless in the face of a deeper hunger that will not be satisfied

**Eight of Nine** *(shocked)*
How can you, a mere Child, know of such hungers of either sort!!?

**Troubadour 1**
He can, because his home is his Essence, that realm of Being made personal by his journey into life. The difference is that you can watch your hungers perform, whereas he cannot. He lives in the eternity of the moment, lost in the fullness of being - a fullness that escapes you and leaves you constantly longing. Thus, he is both more and less than you are . . .

**Nine of Nine** *(takes the hand of Eight of Nine and kisses it softly with love)*
Permit me this, for sometimes a gesture carries what words will not. You are a beautiful and accomplished woman, but I also know of the fires of hunger within you, for they burn within me, too. But I know something of love and what lies beyond it. That path can point the way to the place of gentle immersion that fulfils all hunger. Let me share this with you and we may yet find such peace together.

**One of Nine** *(angry again and shouting at Troubadour 1 in jealousy)*
Hah, so much for your sentiment of being his Queen! Already, I would have to fight for HIS bed! Where is the peace in this supposedly sacred chamber now?

**Troubadour 2**
My brother spoke of a deeper love, as does the King, your Highness. Your place in his arms is already written into the hidden stonework of this building . . .

**One of Nine** *(mutters)*
Foolish dreamers. Let this storm abate, dear God, then we can be on our way!

**Two of Nine** *(studying the King)*
You are a strange man . . so much hidden behind the sobriety of those eyes, so much seen and done, and yet you hide it so.

**Nine of Nine**

And now I can hide it no longer. The escape from the storm was no escape at all, but a plunging into this melee of confrontation and agonies.

You of all people, understand struggle and hunger. Do you think that I hungered to be stood here, naked before all, yet given the role of uniting you into something I do not even know the shape of?

**Troubadour 1**

The shape is below your feet, noble King. Let it speak to the very heart of you and all will be well. When the forces come, which they soon will, you will be their equal, and the chalice of your great being will emerge, ready and cleansed from this fire, to hold steady the Flames of Transformation which will embrace all those here. But first they must be ready in themselves.

**Child**

Great King - the sea beneath that vast cliff is worth the fall. There is life, there is purpose and there is the greatest peace you can ever know.

**Nine of Nine** *embraces the Child, thanking him.*

I do not know what brought me here, but I am glad that your gentle and seeing presence accompanies me. Thank you!

*Two of Nine sits.*

*Child takes the King to stand before Five of Nine (who rises)*

**Child** *(quotes)*

"On crystal tower and legend's stage his voice is lost in honest rage"

Here is one who is appears to be the most safe, the most secure, but whose lot is to be among the saddest. This Miser who makes his life into a Tower of remoteness so that he can watch those below, yet remain uninvolved!

**Five of Nine** *(calmly, and refusing to be drawn into the emotion)*

There is wisdom in such action, Child. You have not yet seen the destruction that the world can heap on a man or woman. The King is wise to speak of the power of ruin, yet it seems he is prepared to risk it once more!

**Troubadour 2**

Perhaps he senses the approach of the hour when the price of true liberation will be ALL that he possesses?

**Five of Nine**

Then he will be foolish.

One should always keep back what is important. Do the very lessons of our childhood not teach us that we must fend for ourselves in all things - and having thus filled our coffers should we open the gates and give it away! My heart shrieks at the very prospect!

**Child**

It is not your heart that shrieks, but your desire to Keep that which you have taken from the world.

**Troubadour 2** *(speaking to Five of Nine)*

Merchant! When I first heard you speak, a clear and present picture came into my mind. The picture was of a fast-flowing stream on a high hillside, dancing in the sunshine as it laughed its happy journey downwards towards the sea from which it would be born again in the eternal joy of Being. Then I saw you in that landscape: the stream bank had been kicked down into the water as though deliberately; the resulting barrier had trapped some of the pure water into a side-flow, which, every hour became more dirty and mud-filled. Your life could be the glittering stream, but your avarice is the mud that traps the flow of true life. That dank liquid is not freedom; it is not even freedom from fear - it is slow death.

**Five of Nine** *(draws himself up angrily, stung by what he knows to be true)*

How dare you! How can you speak for another Mind in that way? How do you KNOW?

**Troubadour 1**

She knows, dear friend, because she has lived for years in the joy of that Stream, and anything that is not of its Essence is clear to her - or in your case - muddy. Do not be offended, but hear her words, for all our sakes! *Five of Nine lapses into silence. He hangs his head.*

*Nine of Nine puts his right hand on the Merchant's shoulder, comfortingly.*

**Nine of Nine**

Dear friend in this Quest. Do not be offended. It would appear that we are all here to change, that we have entered on a Path whose very nature is the painful fire of renewal. Be with us in this, for in this unsettling process, you are not alone.

*Five of Nine nods his head silently.*

*(Child takes Nine of Nine along the direct path from point 5 to point 7. Seven of Nine rises as they approach)*

**Child** *(quotes)*

"In courtly wealth and gilded pride, no song within their toughened hide"

Here is the other half of that twin sentence, great King. He of Courtly Wealth stands before you, assured of his place in the world, which is to TAKE.

**Seven of Nine** *(unruffled)*

I take what I must. As one of Royal Blood, you would know that such a one, ensuring the finances of a kingdom, cannot expect to be popular.

**Troubadour 2**

But can he be popular with himself?

**Seven of Nine**

That is simply a foolish notion. I do what I have to do to fulfil my role and nothing more. I do not even feel the need to ask myself whether I like it or not.

**Troubadour 1**

But there are other things you like very much, Lord Chancellor.

**Seven of Nine**

Why yes! *(smiles self-indulgently)*, there are many pleasures that come with high rank. Good food, the pleasures of the body and mind, and the joy of being served. I find it all very pleasant, but I have worked to gain my present office!

**Troubadour 2**

Indeed you have, but like the Merchant before you, you have diverted the living birds of the mind and turned them into quantity, not seeing them die before you in their gilded cage. .

**Seven of Nine**

Most of my little birds have been very happy in their gilded cages. Cages can be very opulent.

**Troubadour 1**

And did your children think so, too?

**Seven of Nine** *(flashing anger)*

What gives you the right to be do damnably insolent! You have no office, save your self-appointed wanderings, a mere minstrel! My children lived good lives until they were taken from me by accident . . How could you know anything of their lives and their suffering.

**Troubadour 2**

It is your suffering we speak of, Lord Chancellor. The thousand thoughts of grief hidden behind the mask of plenty and control that you wear. You were not always like this! Once, the wellspring of real youth flowed, unblocked, in your being.

**Nine of Nine**

Friend of high office. It is not easy to gaze back and see the Ruin of what we once were. But I am learning that the very vision of ruin is potent in its power to create ACTION. And I see in your angry and hurt words, that there lies a very different Lord Chancellor beneath these softly cultivated expressions of content. Do not be angry with the Troubadours for speaking the Truth.

**Seven of Nine**

But that was too close to– *(is cut off by Eight of Nine speaking)*

**Eight of Nine**

–To the Truth behind your mask, Lord Chancellor? I share with you the passions of the appetites, but we both know that they find their greatest expression in running away

*Seven of Nine glares at Nine of Nine, panting with inner turmoil.*

**Seven of Nine** *(to Eight of Nine)*

And you think this mad journey along the paths of our very beings will change that?

**Eight of Nine**

I would turn that around and ask if you have ever found anything in your deepest hungers that did?
**Seven of Nine** *(softly, giving way to the pain within)*
No
**Eight of Nine**
So what have we to lose, dear friend?
**Seven of Nine** *(almost a whisper, but loud enough to hear)*
Nothing .
*Nine of Nine puts his right hand on the shoulder of Seven of Nine.*
We must be together in this. I can see now that the road to freedom follows the valley of sorrows, at least for a short while, till we learn to look upwards and not at our feet.
*Seven of Nine sits.*
*Technician plays the sound of the Thunderstorm for ten seconds, Queen carries on through this)*
**One of Nine** *(ignoring the thunderstorm, stands and shouts)*
You can be together on your own, you bunch of scoundrels! I want no part of your chess games! I *(chokes on her words)* I am not made of stuff to be moulded by others. I have triumphed over my weaknesses already!
*(Child moves quietly around the circle, clockwise to stand in the West, just before the Guardian. He stops and faces the East, ready to try to block the Queen's coming exit)*
*When Child starts to move, Nine of Nine starts to go towards One of Nine, but she moves determinedly around the enneagram (in the sequence 1-4-2-8-5-7 and back to 1) to evade him.*
*The King stops pursuing her at point One to wait for her return. At each point in the enneagram, she slashes her arms outwards to indicate a cutting of ties to them all.*
*Returning to point One, she pushes the King aside and takes the outer circle to the West, where she finds the Child blocking her way.*
**One of Nine**
Out of my way, strange and warped creature!
*(she pushes him aside, then turns to face the East one last time)*

There, I have banished you all from my life. Now damn the storm! My boots will carry me safely out of this madhouse!

*Guardian opens the doors*

*(she pushes past the Guardian who has opened the doors to let her exit. Then he reseals them, but does not fully close the door)*

*(there is a pause then Keeper 1 breaks the Silence)*

**Keeper 1**

It sometimes happens that the balance of power in a sacred chamber like this is too much for one of the individuals to bear. In this case, the Queen, who was to be at the very heart of our Work together, has felt this intensity and has not been able to bear it.

We must not despair. Despair is the enemy of hope and resolution. There may, yet, be a way forw ...*(breaks off as there are four loud knocks at the temple door - actually carried out by the Queen - One of Nine, who has been listening to the script through the partly open door)*

**Nine of Nine**

Perhaps the Queen returns?

**Troubadour 1**

No, dear King. That knock is from another, and signals a different kind of storm!

My friends, I fear it is too late. Our work was designed to attract they who would empower us on our inner journey. It has been successful.. too successful, for now they have answered, but we lack a Chalice, a container for the female energy that ensures the change of dimension that we seek.

We need not answer the knocking now, but, like the call from the higher powers in our lives, we may ignore it only once. When it knocks at the temple door again, we must open to it or our spiritual lives will perish.

**Keeper 1**

Troubadours, it falls to you to complete this cycle of workings. I am sorry that the beautiful flower we had tried to make for all is now flawed. Please do what you can to make a fitting vessel from what remains.

Let us all take our leave and seek refreshment. The arrival of the Powers, tomorrow, will tax us all, and when the knock comes again, the temple doors must be opened, whether we are ready or not. And do not be consoled too easily, for the Angel of Life is also the taker of Souls.

*Technician plays music for the exits of the companions.*
*The Nine leave the temple, led by Four of Nine.*
*Then the Keepers, then the Upholders.*
*Then the Troubadours.*
*The Technician and the Guardian are the last to leave.*
*On leaving, each salutes the Guardian and the East.*

## *End ritual 4*

# The Return of the Queen
## Ritual Drama 5

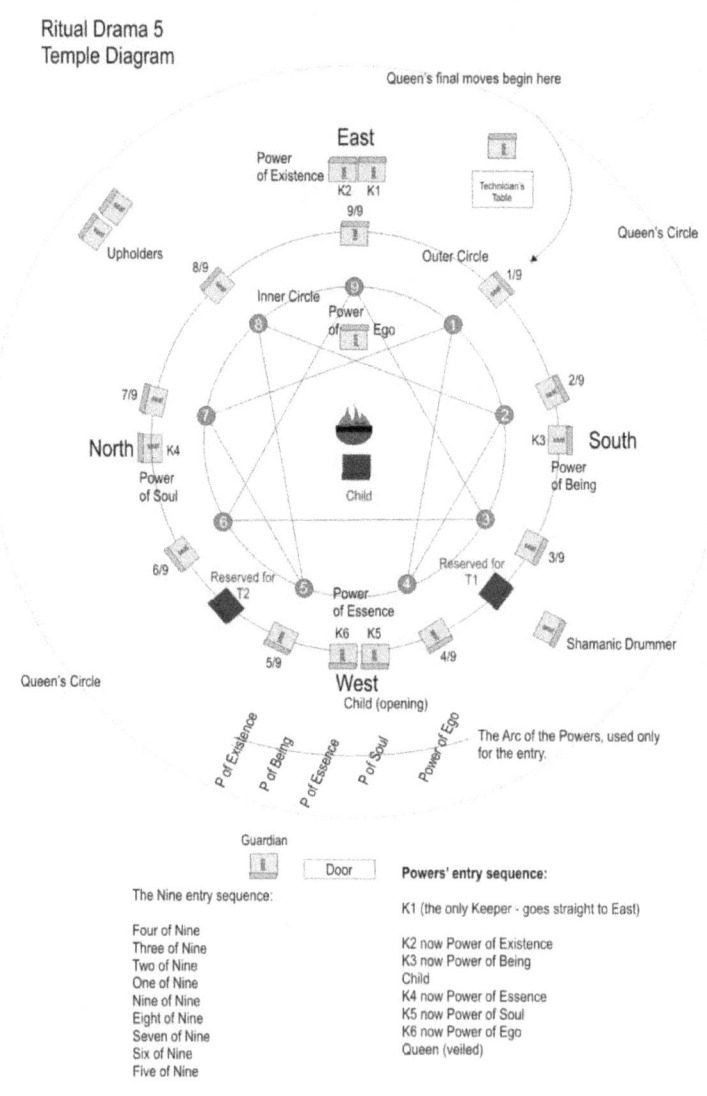

Ritual Drama 5
Temple Diagram

The Nine entry sequence:

Four of Nine
Three of Nine
Two of Nine
One of Nine
Nine of Nine
Eight of Nine
Seven of Nine
Six of Nine
Five of Nine

Powers' entry sequence:

K1 (the only Keeper - goes straight to East)

K2 now Power of Existence
K3 now Power of Being
Child
K4 now Power of Essence
K5 now Power of Soul
K6 now Power of Ego
Queen (veiled)

## Preparation

Queen needs veil.
Cushion for Child.
Guardian needs staff.

The temple is laid out as in the diagram
Note:
Extra chair for Power of Ego, next to Child, East of Flame.
Role allocations
Power of Existence - As Keeper 2, sits in East
Power of Being - as Keeper 3, sits in South
Power of Essence - as Keeper 4, sits in West
Power of Soul - as Keeper 5 - sits in North
Power of Ego - as Keeper 6 - sits with Child East of the flame, as shown in diagram.

## Robing:

All nine of Nine are in white robes or Shells.
The remaining Keeper is in a black robe
The powers are in White Robes, with an orange sash gathered across the right shoulder and tied at the waist.
Only Keeper 1 remains as a Keeper for this ritual and goes to their usual place in the East.
The rest of the Keepers assume the roles of the Powers.
Note:
The Queen (One of Nine) enters veiled and at the end of the line of the Powers. Initially, she stands quietly in the West, but near to the Northern Wall.
When the Powers have made their speeches and are sitting, she begins a continuous slow walk around the very outer circle of the temple until her cue, later in the ritual.

# The Ritual Begins

*Technician plays Monastery bells (to end), loud enough for all to hear through the doors. Technician Plays Chanting, then fades down when all are seated.*
*The upholders enter the temple first and are seated. Then all Nine of Nine enter and take their positions on the outer circle and are seated.*
*The Child is not present. The single Keeper goes to the East and is seated*
*The Troubadours enter and go directly to their positions in the outer circle, as per R4. The Guardian is at his station at the Western door.*

**Keeper 1** *(rises)*
Guardian. Tile the temple so that we may complete our work.
**Guardian** *(seals the temple)*
The temple is, once more, made sacred and secure, Keeper of the First Flame.
**Keeper 1**
Thank you Guardian, for all your work, here.
*(Guardian bows back to Keeper)*
**Keeper 1**
Drummer! I feel we have need of the fortitude carried in your rhythms. Please grace us one last time by censing our sacred Temple with your rhythms.
*Drummer censes the temple.*
**Keeper 1** *(addresses One of Nine, who stands and moves into his 9/9 position)*
Noble King, you now face a difficult task and one that may carry grave risks. Are you prepared to unite the forces in this room without the help of the one who should have been your Queen?
**One of Nine**
If the Troubadours will assist me, I am ready to try. There are many noble souls in this chamber and they deserve that leadership in this Quest.
**Keeper 1**
Then let us begin . . . but where is the Child?

**Troubadour 1**
We do not know, Keeper of the First Flame. We thought he had been taken and protected by you?
**Keeper 1**
No, though that did occur to me. And yet I feel he is in no danger. Do you not sense this also?
**Troubadour 2**
We do, Keeper. Perhaps he was not so easy to dismiss as the Queen supposed and is with her now?
**Keeper 1**
It may be so - Guardian, knock on the door one time, let us see if we have begun this rite without him and he waits outside?
*Guardian strikes the door from inside, once. Immediately there are Four loud knocks from the outside (carried out by Keeper 2, now acting as the Power of Existence)*
**Keeper 1**
I am sorry, Troubadours, but our time has run out. The Powers are here, and they have arrived at a time that will stress us the most - it is often the way with the Spiritual Life.
Do you feel able to help the King in his most noble of quests, even though the danger to him may spill over to you?
**Troubadour 2**
We do, Keeper. We know you must stand aside for this.
*Keeper 1 sits.*
**Troubadour 2**
Guardian, open the West gate of the temple and let in the Inner Lights of Origin, known to the world as the Powers of the Flame.
*Guardian opens the Gates wide and bows to the incoming Powers.*
*They enter in the sequence Existence, Being, Essence, Soul, Child, Ego. And stand in an arc just past the Guardian in the West (see diagram) with the Child slightly towards the East in the centre of the arc.*
*The Troubadours turn to face them.*
**Troubadour 1**
Great Beings, be known and welcome here *(both Troubadours bow)*

*Power of Existence bows slightly back to the Troubadours, then scans the temple.*
**Power of Existence**
You are not ready for us Troubadours! The balance of Life in this temple is precarious! Do you know the risks you face if you go ahead with this Rite?
**Troubadour 1**
We do, great Being. Please know that we have given all we have to be here and dare not go back now.
**Power of Existence** *(smiles slightly)*
You were foolish when you were a child, too.
*Troubadour 1 smiles back and bows.*
**Power of Existence**
Then so be it! In the name of the all-loving let us begin and speak of Origin.
The Child is in our keeping now. You have held him safe and honoured your pledge and we thank you all; but that which he needs is beyond your reach, though today may bring you closer. Child, go and sit by the flame, and watch and learn.
*(Child goes directly via the West and sits on his cushion, facing the Flame, but this time facing Eastwards).*
**Power of Existence** *(holds out their right hand with the fingers spread and walks from the West to the Flame saying:)*
Let us speak of Origin, and of Existence.
The Human Consciousness is the zenith of one third of Creation. The whole Creation has a Will, and a Design for its own Unfoldment. To hold these it must have a Cosmic Chalice, and this we call Existence. Into this Chalice is poured the loving intelligence of Being, which is the One Thing which pervades and is, ALL.
*(Power of Existence spins clockwise with arms raised to embrace the ALL, then moves, directly to sit in the East, next to Keeper 1)*
**Power of Being** *(holds out their right hand with the fingers spread and walks to the Flame saying:)*
Let us speak of Origin, and of Being.

Being is without beginning and end. This flowing, loving, intelligence is the basis of everything we know. Whatever level of consciousness we attain, it will only reveal the greater and greater depth of Being that has always been there within us and before us.

Being also forms the objects that we believe are separated from us. But the Reality and the Truth are that we live and have our own being in a sea of endless loving energy that is our true home. There is no separation, there is in the end, no journey; there is only realisation, and seeing. What unveils itself before us, was always there.

*(Power of Being spins clockwise with arms raised to embrace the ALL, then moves, directly to sit in the South)*

**Power of Essence** *(holds out their right hand with the fingers spread and walks to the Flame saying:)*

Let us speak of Origin, and of Essence.

As Being seeks to fulfil its promise to Existence, it evolves to embrace consciousness on all levels. The Glory of Individual existence comes in to being, and with it, the self-conscious light that is the Human Essence. Born of the full power of Being and never separated from it in foundation, the Glory of Essence moves into creation and lives, incarnate.

*(Power of Essence spins clockwise with arms raised to embrace the ALL, then moves, directly to sit in the West.)*

**Power of Soul** *(holds out their right hand with the fingers spread and walks to the Flame saying:)*

Let us speak of Origin, and of The Soul.

As individual Essence seeks to fulfil its promise to Being, the Soul is created as the evolving substance of Essence, a divine Harvester in which the Human may store and evaluate the lessons of life. The evolved human may use Soul like a mariner uses a ship, to travel between the layers of coming-into-being, or Unfoldment of the divine plan, in the very heart of each moment, in the fire of the Moment, in the Now.

*(Power of Soul spins clockwise with arms raised to embrace the ALL, then moves, directly to sit in the North)*

**Power of Ego** *(holds out their right hand with the fingers spread and walks to the Flame saying:)*
Let us speak of Origin, and of Ego, the Personality.
Being responds to the Ultimate Will of the Creator by pushing itself into the final level of creation, the Physical World.
Now constructed into vehicles of denser and more solid Form, the Power of Being, acting through Essence and Soul, now enters the world of incarnated matter, the densest of all the worlds, and the final act in the Cosmic Drama of unfolding Glory.
Within this garden of intricate density, God wills that there be an Eye, that the full creation may see itself in all its loving and complete glory. The way is hard and long, and there is much suffering because the vision of love and belonging is lost to the developing consciousness, with only a ghost remaining, to ever remind it of its true home.
Locked into the laws of the physical, the Child, lacking the perfect parents that will one day be born, can only learn by Reacting; and in that Reaction it learns Fear, Separation and Despair. But all of Life conspires to provide gaps in the seemingly solid walls of matter, through which to let shine the light of love and being.
The Ego is the muddied set of nine lenses that the Creator longs to wipe clear, but in their creation is also the map of the returning Soul, and the wise can read, in their own frailty, their way home, if they will just learn to See.
This coming into being is the Truth, this journey inwards may be made on the wings of the Soul, if there is bravery and determination in the Heart. Action is all-important, but it is not what it seems!
*(Power of Ego spins clockwise with arms raised to embrace the ALL, then moves, directly to stand behind the Child with their arms on the Child's shoulders; then continues speaking:)*
This Child is very special. Once in a hundred years, one such as this is born, and the Ego does not develop. This means that the Child sees and Speaks from direct knowledge of Essence, and thereby has living dialogue with Being.
Cherish these moments with him, for we must soon take him away

again and protect his fragile existence in the harsh physical world!

But study what is before you in this special Soul, and ask yourself if there is not still a very special child locked within YOU; a child much younger than you, because such life can only take place in the Conscious Present. To do this should be your daily goal, for only in the Present, in the Now, can the glory of Being do its work, opening the path of the most loving and most powerful action within your lives.

*All the Powers close their eyes in prayer for one minute. Absolute silence must be maintained. At the end of one minute, the Power of Existence speaks:*
*The Powers remain standing.*

**Power of Existence**

And now we are all PRESENT. Now the power and the glory are manifest, but beware their forces for they are like a roaring flame that will consume.

Troubadours! You spoke of one who had taken on the task of uniting the Body of Light in this chamber?

*The King (Nine of Nine) stands. All his fellow Pilgrims stand to support him.*

**Troubadour 1**

Yes, great Being. The King before you has raised himself to this task. I pray that you will help him in this, for he knows that his armour is flawed, that his army is untrained, and that his family is incomplete. Despite this, he marches towards the Fire.

**Power of Existence**

Then we shall honour his bravery, but we cannot fully control the wild flame that now waits, nascent, in this chamber. Does he know this?

**Nine of Nine**

Yes, Lord. I know what I am doing. If my life ends now, it will have ended well. For the first time in many years, I am truly alive.

**Power of Being**

Then the special powers in this sacred chamber are yours to command, King. Use them wisely. Show us what you have learned. Build us a living pathway into which the Fire may be poured, as a sword is forged in the mould and hammered into shape on the anvil.

All life is drama, played out against the backdrop of both love and inevitable suffering. Show us you understand the Cosmic Drama, bring it alive in this place. Let all those here help you, for you play with your very lives.

**Nine of Nine** *(bows to the Powers of Existence and Being)*
*(Turns to the vacant spot where, One of Nine, his Queen, is absent.)*
There was one there I would have chosen to be my mate and co-ruler. She was arrogant and strong, but made of fine stuff. She pursued Perfection in all things, although it masqueraded as anger much of the time. This is a lack I cannot fill.
*(Three of Nine comes forward slowly along the direct line to Nine of Nine)*

**Three of Nine**
Great King, if you will have me do this, I will stand in for your Queen. My talents are puny compared to her depth of Being, but I willingly offer myself, even my life, to see you complete this song of transformation.
*(Nine of Nine embraces Three of Nine, then takes her to stand on One of Nine's place, speaks softly and lovingly to her)*

**Nine of Nine** (King)
Brave Dancer. I am overwhelmed by what you have offered and done. Stand then with me here. Let us see if the glory of a soul's highest effort, given in sacrifice, will sway the Powers to help us.
*(Nine of Nine now moves along the line from the position of One of Nine to Four of Nine)*
Lowly Actor, spinner of fine and tragic tales, let us begin the Alchemy of Transformation with you. I have studied you, and I see that, although you are riddled with Envy, you have a heart that is true; and that beneath that veneer, formed by neglect in your childhood, you are really a being who loves the good fortune of others.
*(King places his right hand on the head of Four of Nine, in blessing)*
Begone, envious shadow! Let the light shine from the Being within who, transforming the outer, will show us the brightness of loving appreciation of all.

*(Nine of Nine now moves along the line from the position of Four of Nine to Two of Nine)*

Proud Physician! How skilled you are! But how large is your sense of self-importance. But I have watched you and know that your heart is good and true, and that you long to throw off this crown of anguish and false importance, that you long to be just another traveller on the way, and that this is why you pursued the path of the Pilgrim.

*(King places his right on the head of Two of Nine, in blessing)*

Begone, proud and heavy shadow! Let the light shine from the Being within who, transforming the outer, will show us the joy and the freedom of Humility in the face of the glory that surrounds us each waking second.

*(Nine of Nine now moves along the line from the position of Two of Nine to Eight of Nine)*

Deadly Lady of the Circus, how your hunger and lust for all things in life swept me away when I first heard you speak! But as I watched those energies writhing in you, I saw something else, a gentle young girl, whose innocence was torn away from her in a time far gone, and is covered now with the detritus of life. But that gentle light and heartbeat are there still and I call them forth!

*(King places his hand on the head of Eight of Nine, in blessing)*

Begone, lustful shadow! Let the light shine from the Being within who, transforming the outer, will show us the treasure of Innocence in the face of the glory that surrounds us each waking second.

*(Nine of Nine now moves along the line from the position of Eight of Nine to Five of Nine to whom he points in mock aggression)*

Mean and controlling figure who sits atop his own tower of detachment! *(pauses)* But you are not, dear friend. Beneath that detached image, you are fearful of loss - that what has been gained or given you will be all there is. And so you hoard it, living from moment to moment in the dread of its removal, thereby bathing in stagnation and slime instead of the waters of living life, which are always bubbling over and through you like a brook, ever ready to bathe and nourish you!

*(King places his hands on the head of Five of Nine, in blessing)*
Begone, Shadow of Avarice! Let the light shine from the Being within who, transforming the outer, will show us the power that non-attachment brings into a lifetime, as it frees the Soul to truly BE in the moment, without fetters.
*(Nine of Nine now moves along the line from Five of Nine to Seven of Nine)*
Our Lord Chancellor - noble of bearing and a very rich man, indeed! Or is he? For all his ability to manipulate the world so that it constantly feeds him, inside is he not desperately afraid that the feeding will stop, that all his talents will prove useless in the wave of famine that he will not be able to control? This fear, grounded so deep in his mind and emotions, and now totally unseen, drives his moves in the world so, that if he cannot wind in the food in larger and larger portions, he feels a hunger that cannot possibly be real!
Dear Friend, how shared are all of these fixities of our minds, how real are these phantoms on which we base our movements in the world?
*(King places his hand on the Chancellor's shoulder in a gesture of friendship)*
When did you last dance, naked and unfed, without a care in the world, in that high stream in the sunshine of your former life?
*(Lord Chancellor, hangs his head, and sobs, the King takes his opportunity and, breathing deeply, places his right hand on the Chancellor's head, in blessing)*
**Technician** *(look for cue in next paragraph)*
Begone, Shadow of Gluttony! Let the light shine from the Being within who, transforming the outer, will show us the power that freedom from false hunger brings into a lifetime, as it unshackles the Soul to truly BE in the moment, without appetite.
*The King turns around to face the flame,*
*(MUSIC cue, five seconds only) then recoils slightly as he feels its increased power.*
*(The Queen,* **One of Nine**, *travelling around the outer circle clockwise, now stops at the outer North position, the point of Darkness, and waits, judging her timing so that she can re-enter the enneagram at her position (One of Nine) as below:*
**Nine of Nine (King)** *(continues, but standing by Seven of Nine)*
I have done what I can. I have tried to show them that we are not separate, that our lives are truly shared.

I can do no more, yet I sense that the gate of power that now opens before me has another behind it. My eyes are opening anew, and see the glories beyond, but my skills are not fledged and I don't have the key to control this wave of energy that now comes at me. (Fights the energy from the flame, shielding his eyes)
*(King looks desperately to his original, true companions, the Dancer and the Fugitive)*
Dearest of companions, you who embarked on this mad quest with me at the outset, come and be with me now, for I fear my strength is failing!
*(Dancer moves directly from her present position at One of Nine (the Queen's position), and the Fugitive moves from his position at Six of Nine, both travel the direct lines to join the King at Seven of Nine, as they arrive, the King begins to slump, and they hold him up)*

**Dancer (Three of Nine)**
Great Powers, who have shown us such wonder, can you not intervene and help us now? This brave warrior is overwhelmed, yet what he has done is right and just!

**Fugitive (Six of Nine)**
I have lived in Fear all my life, but I have always run away from it. This great King, this mighty heart, walked right into the centre of it, for us all! Please help him!

**Power of Existence**
The laws under which we operate are directly from the Creator. It is not a question of desire or wish or even Will. We cannot intervene to help the Son unless the Father and Mother are united. Together they can hold the power that brings on the birth of the truly new, their Son. She alone can use the Power to shape the Horizon. Your great forebears understood this when they gave the world the legend of Isis and Osiris, and their son, Horus.
*(Dancer (Three of Nine) refuses to give up and pulls the failing King along the line to One of Nine. The Fugitive helps her. They arrive at Point One of Nine and, there, support the King's weight)*

*(At this point the Queen should be in the outer East and now faces West, ready to "descend" onto the ring of the Enneagram at her station, 1/9.*
*Technician (cue in next paragraph)*
**Dancer** *(gazing at the Fire)*
I can do this, I know I can be more than I am. I will Transform this energy and give my life for the King. Fugitive, take him, bear his weight while I try this!
*Technician plays the flame noise loudly, 3 seconds*
*(Fugitive holds the King, Dancer takes two steps directly towards the flame, and cries out, unable to hold the increased power without the protection of the enneagram structure)*
**Dancer**
I cannot! I am feeble in the face of this! (she slumps to the floor, dying from the overload of energy)
*(The Queen enters the enneagram at One of Nine and rips off her veil. She looks at the dying Dancer)*
**Queen (One of Nine)**
Enough! I have never seen my folly written so painfully on the world before. Now I WILL stop this!
*(Queen walk directly from point One of Nine to where the Dancer lies fallen, and, kneeling, takes her in her arms.)*
**Queen (One of Nine)**
Brave woman, who has shown me what is truly remarkable in the race called SHE. You do not need to die to bring this stupid Queen to her senses. *(shaking her own head, Queen continues: )*
Begone arrogance, begone anger. Open, eyes, and see the beauty of this sacrifice and be baptised into this new land with your own tears!
*Queen helps Dancer to her feet and they stagger back to position One of Nine, where Fugitive (Six of Nine) takes her from the Queen - she is seen to recover. The Queen turns to the King.*
Brave heart. In your indolence, I found disgust. In your Love for others, I have found inspiration and a new beginning. In your Action, I have found Love. Will you take me as your Queen?
**King** *(exhausted but elated)*

My heart sings at the thought. But there is still work to do, and I know that only you can do it!

**Queen** *turns to the Power of Existence in the East.*

Great Power of Existence, if I heard your words well, then the Chalice stands before you. I am ready to serve those in this room. Show me how I can.

**Power of Existence**

Your readiness is seen and loved. But you cannot act on my level. I will pass you to my brothers and sisters in Time. *(He points to the Power of Being in the South).*

*Queen turns to the Power of Being in the South.*

**Queen (One of Nine)**

I am ready, great Power. Will you direct me?

**Power of Being**

I am ready to receive you, awakened Queen, but you must travel to me, with your King; and the chariot for you both must be fashioned from what happens next. For that you need to pass to my brothers and sisters in Space. *(He points to the Power of Essence in the West).*

*Queen turns to the Power of Essence in the West.*

**Queen (One of Nine)**

I am ready, great Power. Will you direct me?

**Power of Essence.**

I am ready to receive you, awakened Queen, but you must be joined with your King; and to achieve that marriage, you must take this company from the outer to the inner. For that you need to pass to my brothers and sisters. *(She points to the Power of Soul in the North*

*Queen turns to the Power of Soul in the North.*

**Queen** (One of Nine)

I am ready great Power. Will you direct me?

**Power of Soul** *(smiling)*

I cannot direct you, for you have become me, and you stand in the eternity that is the true Present. Now you must search for that which is imperfect and transform it one level deeper than the King did.

Take him with you and find the impure, he has already begun to change the base metal into Gold. Now begin your journey, for the hour is late. *(Says nothing more, but points to the floor of point One of Nine)*
*The Queen turns to the Dancer and the Fugitive.*

## Queen (One of Nine)

Go quickly to your places, my thanks cannot be expressed in the seconds that I feel we have left - but they will be, later, should we all survive this inferno. For now, take my love and blessing with you both, in the Kingdom that is dawning, you will be counted among the highest, and many will record how Vanity was transformed into Truth and Harmony; and Fear was transformed into Courage and then Strength!

*(Fugitive takes Dancer back along the circle of the enneagram to her home point Three of Nine Then he proceeds along the direct line to his station at Six on Nine. Both face the Queen.*

## Nine of Nine (King)

Troubadours! Help us in this. What is my Queen to do? I have walked the pattern of eternity and done what I can. But I can see no way to further transform those in this room.

## Troubadour 1

You have done exactly what you could do, noble King, and in so doing, have transformed yourself not only into a ruler of Action, but also revealed your deepest nature, which is Love. You are already transformed in the eyes of everyone but yourself, but that will come with Reflection. .

## Troubadour 2

The Queen must now finish this highest of rites. She can see what you cannot. By coming into her inner nobility when looking at your sacrifice, she has already seen that there is a deeper world beyond the virtues that you laid bare with your brave sweep of this chamber. She belongs to that level - yours is the land of Action, made whole by your enduring Love. It is to her, in the world of Formation that the final task falls of revealing the innermost core of all those here, and the reasons they lost their former estates.

**Troubadour 1**
When this is done, the barriers and the boundaries will fall away, and something that happened here will be recorded forever in the annals of the wise. Noble Queen, go to your task, for it lies in your power alone!
*Queen (One of Nine) Looks down at the floor, preparing herself, then raises herself straight and breathes deeply.*

**Queen (to King)**
Go to your station, my love. I must complete this as alone as you were. Pray for me, and that we are re-united at the ending.
*King embraces her, silently, then returns along the circle directly (anti-clockwise) to position Nine of Nine.*
*Queen goes to face Four of Nine*

**Queen (One of Nine)**
Poor player. But, how deeply the King saw when he looked into your Soul and there shone back the light of Stability and Composure. But there is a layer yet deeper, one which once connected the very core of you to the unchanging and eternal qualities of Being. In this inner world, you are already crowned with knowing your deepest sense of Origin, and I call you forward into this new land wearing this crown.
*Queen embraces Four of Nine, then moves to stand facing Two of Nine*
Proud Physician. But, how deeply the King saw when he looked into your Soul and there shone back the light of Humility, washing away the falseness of Pride with its effortless Grace. But there is a layer yet deeper, one which once connected the very core of you to the unchanging and eternal qualities of Being. In this inner world, you are already crowned with knowing the majesty of the Cosmic Will, and working with it rather than in isolation, with a false sense of Self. See how you have truly become yourself by surrendering to the greater Will. I call you forward into this new land wearing this crown.
*Queen embraces Two of Nine, then moves to face Eight of Nine*
Ferocious Tyger Lady!. But, how deeply the King saw when he looked into your Soul and there shone back the light of Innocence, washing away the falseness of perpetual Lust.

But there is a layer yet deeper, one which once connected the very core of you to the unchanging and eternal qualities of Being. In this inner world, you are already crowned with knowing the very essence of the Cosmic Truth, that All is one thing, and that the wild thing you had to tame was only yourself, now your deepest inner lover in the dance of unfolding creation. I call you forward into this new land wearing this crown.

*Queen embraces Eight of Nine, then moves to face Five of Nine*

Miserly Merchant, locked in your transparent tower with your treasures!. But, how deeply the King saw when he looked into your Soul and there shone back the gentle peace of non-attachment washing away the falseness of your fear of constant loss. But there is a layer yet deeper, one which once connected the very core of you to the unchanging and eternal qualities of Being. In this inner world, you are already crowned with knowing the very science with which the Creator decides the next moment, to rule across all eternity with a design that is constantly new and which owes nothing to the past, I call you forward into this new land wearing this crown.

*Queen embraces Five of Nine, then moves to stand facing Seven of Nine*

Gluttonous Lord Chancellor! But, how deeply the King saw when he looked into your Soul and there shone back the Gentleness of Sobriety, washing away the falseness of an appetite never assuaged. But there is a layer yet deeper, one which once connected the very core of you to the unchanging and eternal qualities of Being. In this inner world, you are already crowned with knowing the very essence of the Cosmic Wisdom, that all true decisions are made by the Creator and that we become the wisest we can be in line with that greater vision. I call you forward into this new land wearing this crown.

*The Queen turns to face her last path home, looking at the King with love and understanding. As she sets off to walk back to position One of Nine (very slowly), the Powers of Soul and Ego speak, together*

**Power of Soul and Power of Ego speaking together:**

And so it is made whole, by a company of brave souls who, in their hour of trial, knew to face themselves rather than the mere appearance of the world and by a Queen who attained her Perfection in the deepest moments of Serenity.

**Power of Existence** *commands the Queen:*
Come to the King, and turn you both to me, do not worry about the Paths of Power, for they no longer bind you!
*Queen walks to collect the King and they turn to face the Power of Existence*

**Power of Existence**
Power of Being! Do we consider that these two, who have led the Quest, are fit to take each other in Cosmic Marriage?
*Power of Being walks to the flame, gathers its radiance and places left and right hands on the heads of the Queen and King.*

**Power of Being**
We do, and may love and passion for life rule all their days. *(speaks to King and Queen)* Embrace each other, for you are now married in the eyes of the highest and have been judged fit to lead your Kingdom.
*(King and Queen embrace)*

**Power of Essence**
Yet one task remains. Will you take the Child and undertake to raise him in the true Light of the Cosmos, knowing that he must embrace both the physical as well as the spiritual, but he must do so in the light of the Oneness of All.

**King and Queen (together)**
We will.
*Power of Essence comes forward and takes the Child, directly from flame to East, to be with the King and Queen. They embrace him. Then all three face the East and are silent.*

**Keeper 1**
Troubadours, whose selfless service to this company has ensured its success. We thank you, but now another day must dawn and, perhaps, another band of pilgrims comes this way!
*Troubadour 2 moves around the flame and embraces the King, Queen and Child. She bows to them and leaves via the West, bowing to the Guardian, but stopping to wait for the other Troubadour.*

*Troubadour 1 moves around the flame and embraces the King, Queen and Child. He bows to them and leaves via the West, bowing to the Guardian, he and Troubadour 2 are united.*

*As they turn to salute the temple, the Troubadours embrace.*

**Troubadour 1**

It is done. There is new life here. The sun rises.

**Troubadour 2**

Yes dear Brother, but the great wheel turns and so must we! Another day dawns, and the Hawk calls!

*The Troubadours leave the temple.*

*Technician plays music.*

**Keeper 1**

Companions, the storm is over, and the pass to the High Land is open, again. This rite is ended. Take it with you in your hearts and recall it to life when you need it most. Be warmed by the memory that you were here, that you were Present.

**Keeper 1** *continues*

Guardian! We thank you for your duties which were nobly done. For one last time, open the gate of the West and let us depart.

*Guardian opens the temple door.*

**Guardian**

*The temple doors are open, Keeper. The rite is ended.*

*Technician plays, the companions leave to this music.*

*The Powers leave clockwise; followed by the Nine (but not King and Queen, who stay with the Child and are the last to leave).*

*The remaining Keepers leave together with any upholders.*

*Finally the King and Queen leave with the Child.*

*All bow to the Guardian on leaving and salute the East, where a new day is dawning.*

# End Ritual 5

# *Vigil and Dawn*
## The Birth of the Silent Eye School
### By Stuart France

This birthing vigil took place early in the morning on Sunday 21st April, 2013. The vigil began, before the dawn, and continued, just before sunrise on the nearby hillside.

***PREPARATION*:**

The Temple Room will be prepared on the Saturday evening following Ritual Four and prior to Social Time.

A west facing seat will be positioned centrally in the Enneagram for the Mother.

Behind the Mother Seat to the left will be a west facing seat for the Father.

Behind the Mother Seat to the right will be a west facing seat for the Son.

Facing the Mother Seat in line with positions Three and Six of the Enneagram the Seat of Offering will be placed.

All the other seats will be arranged as wings around the Mother, Father and Son Seats within the Enneagram.

There where will be one seat at the head of the Enneagram (position 9) reserved for the Guardian who enters the temple last.

Chalice/Wine, Platter/Bread, Altar board…

All timings are approximate…

**N.B** This is a very simple and straightforward ritual. We would like to perform this ritual without the use of scripts or devices. To that end the supporters and students will need to familiarise themselves and be fully conversant with the format of the ritual and will need to memorise their affirmations. If difficulties are experienced remembering the affirmations during the ritual Companions will be prompted.

**NOTES**

Silence plays a big role in this ritual.
The easiest way to become silent in a meaningful way is to listen.
If you are listening properly you are silent.
The Vigil never really starts or finishes.
A suitable juncture at which to join the Vigil would be before sleep the previous night.
On waking you continue your Vigil through your ablutions which should be accomplished with a minimum of fuss.
Note and forestall your usual reactions to the daily round and then offer them up to the silence.
Upon meeting, forego verbal greetings to your 'Companions in Silence' - simply nod, or bow, or smile...
By this time our silence as a group will have manifested palpably.
Respect that silence and perpetuate it.
From the depths of silence are great things born.

# *VIGIL*

4.00am Mother enters temple in silent meditation. Son prepares hillside Temple.
4.30 am: Father and Son meet at the Temple Portal.
4.40am: The Father enters the Temple, approaches the Seat of offering, makes his offering and after a short space for Communion with the Mother takes his seat to her left and places his left hand on her shoulder.
4.50am: The Son enters the Temple, approaches the Seat of offering, makes his offering and after a short space for Communion with the Mother takes his seat to her right and places his right hand on her shoulder.
4.55am: The Companions gather at the Temple Portal in Silence...

From 5.00am onwards: each companion enters the Temple alone approaches the Seat of offering, makes offering and after a short space for Communion with the Mother takes any of the seats behind the Mother, Father and Son seats except the seat reserved for the Guardian. The Guardian is to orchestrate the entry of the Companions and ensure their silence. The Guardian enters the Temple last, closes the temple doors, offers and then takes the seat at the head of the enneagram (position 9). When the Guardian has taken his seat, the Father and Son remove their hands from the Shoulder of the Mother and the Silent Vigil is joined...

# *DAWNING*

5.30 am: ...The Mother stands, opens the temple doors, and leaves the temple. The Father, Son and Companions stand and follow in that order... The Guardian exits last and brings up the rear of the procession into the hills.
(note: no verbal signs will be given, the Mother will simply leave. Those who wish to follow need to be ready and observant)
The Mother, followed by the Father and Son enter the Temple antechamber, don cloaks and pick up ritual props. (Mother - Chalice and wine, Father - Platter and bread, Son, Altar Board) They then head out to the Hillside. The Companions who wish to attend don hats and coats in silence and follow them.
The Mother leads the company in silence to a pre-determined location in the hills. This is about a ten-minute walk from the Nightingale centre and is very close.
Upon reaching the Hills, the Father joins the Mother at the head of the group, with the Son behind.
Upon reaching the ritual location the Mother and Father pass their props to the Son, go on ahead and then turn to face the Company holding hands.

The Company should form up into two crescents or semi-circles roughly following the contours of the landscape.

The front crescent should comprise those Companions who are already members of the School or wish to enter the School as students.

The back crescent should comprise the witnesses, upholders or supporters of the school.

Whilst the Crescents are forming the Son Sets up the Altar Board with bread and wine a little to one side of the ritual space and then stands in front of the first crescent facing the Mother and Father.

Mother and Father release hands... stand a little apart... and then in unison... very slowly... raise their arms aloft... in greeting... to the rising sun.

With their arms fully extended they hold for a time...then slowly turn to face each other... and still with arms outstretched... link hands to form an arch overhead.

When the arch is formed the Son takes a step forward, assumes the Osiris posture, with head bent and arms folded over the chest, then raises his head...unfolds his arms... into a gesture of loving acceptance and release... steps forward... and walks through the gateway formed by the bodies and arms of the Mother and Father.

**MOTHER AND FATHER**: (Chant Together)
CCCCCCRRRRRROOOOOOMMMMMMAAAAAATTTTTT
(Cromaat)

Upon passing through the gateway the Son takes out a vial of anointing oil raises it to the rising sun and utters a consecration...

**SON**:
O Lord, may the power of your love infuse this oil may it protect and guide all those anointed with this chrism on this day and forever more ...then turns to face the first crescent of Companions on the other-side of the gateway...

The Companions in the first crescent (who already are or wish to be part of the School) step forward one by one, assume the Osiris posture with head bent and arms folded over the chest, then raise head...unfold arms... into a gesture of loving acceptance and release... step forward... and walk through the gateway formed by the bodies and arms of the Mother and Father as the Son did before them.

**MOTHER AND FATHER**: (Chant Together):
CCCCCCRRRRRROOOOOOMMMMMMAAAAAATTTTTT

After passing through the gateway the companions stop in front of the Son.

**SON:**
Why have you passed through the gates of Light and Life?

**COMPANION:**
I have risen. I have gathered myself together like the beautiful, flame-gold, Hawk of the Sun. RA enters in day by day to hear my words.

**SON:**
(takes anointing oil and traces a circle on the third eye region of the companion's brow with the heart finger, then places a point in the middle of the circle with the thumb, applies pressure and chants):

**SON:**
RRRRRRRRRAAAAAAAAAAAAA. (Ra)

The Son and Companion bow to each other and the Companion then moves to stand behind the Son and eventually forms a crescent as the other companions join.

When all the Companions of the first crescent have passed through the gates of Light and Life the first Companion from the second crescent steps forward... bows... and passes through the gateway to stand before the Son.

**SON**:
Why have you passed through the gates of Light and Life?
**COMPANION**:
Because the One is whole and I bear loving witness to that wholeness.

The Son and Companion bow to each other and the Companion moves to stand behind the son and the first crescent eventually forming a second crescent as the other Companions join.

When all have passed through the gates of Light and Life the Father and Mother lower their arms, retrieve the host and wine, together bless and consecrate them and then serve the companions starting with the Son, then the first... and then the second crescents.

At the end of which the Mother and Father serve each other and then proclaim the school birthed.

The companions with Mother, Father and Son, make their way back to the Nightingale Centre.

### END

A farewell but not goodbye.
Hold us in your hearts as we shall you.
*Steve Tanham, Sue Vincent, Stuart France and the members of the Silent Eye School of Consciousness.*
*21 April 2013*

*The Opening of the Eye*
# *The Companions Tales*

## *A CONVERSATION (overheard)*

*How went the weekend?*
The weekend went well.
*Were I to allow three words as a description could you describe it?*
...
*Think carefully now...*
....Love...Cocoon...Stratosphere...
*Considering the dictum... the first shall be last...the last...first...what did the weekend produce?*
A stratospheric cocoon of love.
*And what is likely to emerge from such a thing?*
Something out of this world!

# The Drama Begins
## Sue Vincent

There had been hugs and welcomes, flurries of suitcases, gorgeously coloured garments peeking shyly from their wrappings, but most of all the joy of meeting old friends, many for the very first time in person.
And then we began.
There was the welcome and a dinner friendlier, warmer, more full of laughter than I have ever seen at one of these gatherings so early in the proceedings. Maybe I am biased... but I was not the only one to remark on the feeling in the air.
We talked through the teaching method and the way the weekend would unfold, then, suddenly it seemed, it was time to begin.
There had been a last minute change of plan, as one of the company could not be there on time. Matt, our fabulous photographer, had stepped in gallantly to cover for most of her role as one of the Keepers of the First Flame, but for some strange reason he did not see himself as Isis. So I had, unexpectedly, opened the drama in the role of the Mother. Not precisely as we had planned, but in the end, it seemed so fitting I could not help but smile as I looked around the circle.
A quick change later then Steve and I, clad in the glorious solar colours of the School, and Stuart, without whom none of this could have ever been the same, were waiting our turn to enter the Temple. And that was quite a moment.
There is an energy to these things that builds slowly through the weekend, becoming deeper and stronger as both drama and understanding unfold, yet this very first moment was filled with a tension and anticipation that was palpable and very moving.
Of course, the companions had probably realised by this point that we were about to sing, Steve and I....and I am not known for my singing, or not in a positive manner anyway....
Yet, it seemed that when Troubadour One took up the guitar and began to sing the song written for this moment, and Troubadour Two stood behind him with her hands on his shoulder and they raised their voices in harmony, as the Child gently woke the Nine from sleep,

something fell into place. The Troubadours sang in tune and the simple music woke more than the sleepers.

A story began to unfold, and with the characters' waking something came alive and began a journey into self-exploration that left none unmoved through the weekend. The ritual drama began to unfold and what seemed a simple story lit up from the inside as the points of the enneagram were brought to life by the archetypal figures so lovingly crafted and beautifully played.

There were experienced ritualists and some for whom this was a first taste, but none who had taken this journey before.

As we filed out in silence, not one was left untouched by the feeling in that room and there was a real reverence as each saluted the simple central Light that symbolises so much. The stairs were lined with white robed figures, quietly waiting for the working space to empty, and that Light was reflected in all eyes.

My mind skipped back to the previous Alchemy weekends here and recognised the thread that ran through them to bring us to this point. Similar, but very different. And then my heart slid forward to the next ritual, the following morning knowing what had been written. If there was so much emotion here already, I could not begin to imagine how that was going to feel.

And I was right.

I could never have imagined such beauty, such warmth, or so much loving joy.

# A Dancer's Tale
## *Alienora Taylor*

All my life I have seen myself as clumsy and cack-handed so, being chosen to play a dancer in this weekend's Silent Eye Birth was confronting, to say the least.

I also wanted to create something tight, beautifully-crafted and perfect to express those days – but, for reasons which I explain in this piece, the journal I wrote during the weekend is going to take the place of more sculpted words. The following quote, taken from a much longer entry for Saturday 20th April, expresses the above:

'We talked, almost continuously, Dean and I, which was great – about, amongst other things, over-reliance upon Facebook and how the lack of contact with the world can be dangerous and damaging on all sorts of levels; how taking a walk, touching earth with feet and hands, feeling the sun on your body, can be so healing and invigorating.

'We also talked about the fact that one cannot truly sort things out through the medium of keyboard to laptop writing. There is something about that loving and creative circle of heart, hand, pen, paper (which, of course, I'm using now!) that communicates soul-truths and the real self in a way tapping upon keys never can…'

*Sunday 21st April – late*

I am back home, looking out at a darkening sky – very tired, having been up since 4 a.m.(!)…but, oh, what a brilliant and happy weekend! As a group, we gelled brilliantly – and a sub-section of the more raucous and rebellious of us (me, Dean, Matt, Kevin, Katie and Jordis) became fast friends and were exceeding loud, bawdy and funny at every meal, firing off hilarious one-liners all over the shop; it was such a relaxed and free bond, almost as if we were siblings!

When we drew up at the back entrance yesterday, Sue, smoking a nervous cigarette and resplendent in tangerine, was there; we hugged and later, when I came back from stashing my stuff in my room, she was waiting for me with a large canvas. And, upon it? The beautiful midnight blacks, purples, silvers and blues of the Dark Wings picture she painted for me a while back. I was incredibly touched, and absolutely love it.

*Dark Wings picture, painted by Sue Vincent, and a gift to me..*

The intensity of the five related ritual dramas (especially the final one in which my character, The Dancer, had to do a dying swan – or, as I put it in my usual self-deprecating way, a dying pterodactyl…) was almost overwhelming and I was in tears as I bowed to the light, to the Guardian and made my way out of the Temple.

It was a journey of the mind, the soul, the body and the emotions. I felt as if I had been flayed, exposed for what I really am – and touched by the breath of the Creator.

There is something very special about the bond which develops during ritual drama (or, indeed, more traditional rites) – the group soul, the intensity of non-verbal communication; the moments of absence (when you are taken over by an inner being, when the ensouling process clicks perfectly into place); the moments when you stop being the observer, step into – and become immersed in – the multi-sensual world of the rite; the two worlds existing side by side: the physical 'reality'(in so far as you can say that) of the Temple – the shape of the Enneagram; the Keepers dotted about, white-robed and orange-sashed; the nine Pilgrims in their places, white-robed with odd splashes of colour (the Actor's mask, the Tyger Lady's fur, the golden cloaks of King and Queen, the Dancer's purple cloak); the Child seated in front of the central light; the tangerine robes of the two Troubadours…

…and, behind it, a strong sense of a vast rocky cavern, deep in the high mountains surrounding the monastery: its echoes and silent susurrations (sensed rather than heard) ; its faint drippings and splashings; its scent of incense and odours of roughly cured wool and sun-dried linen; its chanting of bell and voice; its curious whispers of serenity and stern purpose; its hiding of the Child, the special Child – and its strange detachment from the rest of the world.

…blue, blue skies, I saw, and snow, deep snow, and a hawk soaring overhead.

…very odd sensation, to know the familiarity of wild red hair, white robe, plain rope cord, patterned purple cloak, to watch and grow anxious…

…and then to disappear, for want of a better word, into a different world where a wounded King, bowed down and overwhelmed, lurches across a narrow ridge, near collapse; a cold plain of existence where arms reach instinctively to offer warmth, comfort, succour, support; where the pain of being not-quite-the-best (chosen only because the Queen was absent) was tempered by a genuine love, a real need to help, a willingness to sacrifice, if necessary, EVERYTHING…

…and then the sense of its all being too much, the bitterness of failure, the threat and pain of the scouring radiance of pure flame, the epitome of light – and the agony made manifest (in a scream, I was told later, by those I had inadvertently frightened)…

…and the awful crippling weakness, heaviness, anguish; the once-light dancing feet tethered; the enviable grace toppled by grief's gravity; the bright spirit smothered by overwhelming loss and sadness; the swan wings clipped; the long neck fading upon white soft feathers; the valiant heart beating ever slower; the contrary power of utter lassitude hurling the battered fragments towards the abyss…

Saved. By the Queen. By the rival. The better-than. The rightful consort of the loved one.

'Twas ever thus. Down through the ages. A pattern repeated endlessly – baton passed from girl to girl, century to century, until the lesson is learned , the shape questioned or the pieces rearranged.

And the tears. For the Pilgrim music. The end of the Fellowship. The vessel's inner wounds exposed by the dance. The symmetry and wonder of it all. The wish not to leave the Child, the Keepers, the bright Troubadours, the magical Shamanic Drummer, the Upholders, the familiar tall figure of the Guardian…the wish, above all, to remain in the ritual space, to delay the return to 'real' life…

The memories, of the group canvas now containing many colourful painted images and a paragraph taken from this volume and written in my neatest handwriting; the jamming sessions with the Drummer, him on his Shamanic drums, anklet of bells tinkling-or singing Irish songs; me on fiddle or recorder; Sheila dancing, with pixie ears and elven gait; me playing 'Mad World' on piano, the Drummer singing…

Outrageous laughter down the pub with Allan, Anne, Stuart, Matt, Kevin, Katie and Dean – aching and rolling around! Our final meal, talking about garlic condoms – and the new range of vegetable ones in a more general sense – hilarity springing up from such comments as, 'Bet that's got a big BULB on the end!'

Then, the Iron Age Roundhouse being built outside, in a field, and the invitation to help stomp the floor into being which I, caught in a welter of mud-based childhood memories, was unable to resist.

Watched by the smokers amongst our merry band, I donned a thick black jumper and wellies, tied my hair in a ponytail and sauntered down to the branch-woven structure.

What fun! Clay was heaped in rigid piles, water sprinkled, and the stomp began. Clump, clomp went the welly-clad feet, whilst a bright blue sky smiled knowingly overhead (having seen it all before) and a coldish sun winked through the bare roof space.

Soon, I was mud-spattered and laughing mightily as clay flew everywhere (even, as I discovered later, up my nose!). One of the guys there explained about the way Iron Age man arranged his Roundhouse including, I was delighted to discover, a space, as he put it, '…for burying Granny…' Ah! they did it right in those far-off days. Earth to earth, no messing…and lots of mess!

Eventually (and, perhaps, inevitably), I got stuck, welly-wedged tight in the now-packed clay – but not before 'throwing' a very rough bowl and leaving it on a handy withy to dry. A small child tried to pull me out – and failed! I pulled, heaved and ho'ed…and shot free, with a revolting squelch, leaving both wellies and a sock (rather a fancy black and pink number) behind.

Cold clay paddling was great! Such fun to feel the mud oozing between my toes!

The wellies plopped out; the sock I have donated to the foundations…

Showering took AGES, and I left clay deposits all over the tray at the bottom!

My inner eye now moves to Saturday, early evening – and me, still dressed in robe and purple cloak, posing by stone shed whilst Matt took photos – and then seeing, afterwards, his astonishing image of us all. The nature of it I shall not reveal because it will be shown soon, and I don't want to spoil the surprise. Suffice it to say that, to me, it sums up the weekend better than any words could.

And then I move to the Birth of the school itself: the 4 a.m. waking; Matt knocking on my door to make sure I was ready, bless him; the silent vigil outside the Temple; the sight of the Father, Mother and Son within, and the vigil continued; the Mother rising and leading us all – warmly dressed and still silent – out into the crisply cold air, sunrise's fingers beginning to scratch red streaks upon the sky's skin; the slow measured walk up a track, an inquisitive lamb bleating, gambolling and approaching our voiceless procession; the climb up the hillside to a field ridge below trees; the low-flying hawk appearing at just the right moment...

Then, the laughter as, giddy, tussocks pulled me out of gravity's logic and I trembled all over the grass! The linked arms, hugs and lovely camaraderie...

My love and thanks to everyone there, especially Sue and Steve. It was wonderful, magical, humbling...

And I, no longer constrained by my mind's rigidity of vessel shape, found my Inner Dancer.

# *A Mother's tears*
## Sue Vincent

I was up to meet the dawn on Saturday, finding the world covered in a heavy frost and very beautiful. The morning began with a guided meditation. The companions gathered at 7am and closed their eyes. It was a simple journey... that of a seed thrown by an unseen hand to the winds. The tiny point of consciousness watched from inside itself as it grew, illustrating the journey into becoming.
Breakfast and preparation... and then it was time for the second of the ritual dramas.
These dramatic episodes, played with conviction in a place made sacred, have a profound effect, enabling understanding, engaging the emotions as well as the intellect as they bring the teachings to life in a unique manner. This is one of the ways we will teach, through workshops and teaching sessions and the weekend workshops, open to all.
These do not form an essential part of the School's course, they are not required, nor is attendance limited to School members... but rather they enhance and enrich it, as well as allowing friendships and companionship to grow. Study can be a lonely thing and the personal journey must be ultimately walked alone... but that does not mean there cannot be company along the way, a hand to hold when the ground seems rough or laughter shared in sunlight.
The first ritual drama saw the arrival of nine travellers, sheltering from a storm in the monastery of the Keepers of the First Flame. A shamanic drummer and two Troubadours, accompanied by a strange Child also sought shelter. They were following a quest to rescue an imprisoned king, or so they believed, and sought shelter and refuge for the Child while they continued their journey.
The first drama introduced these characters, and ended as the Troubadours left to continue their search, leaving the Child in the care of the nine and the Keepers. On Saturday morning the second drama

was to explore the characters further, seeing deeper into their innermost being.

As the Troubadours were 'absent', Steve assisted our technician and had placed me in the role of the Great Mother, simply to bless the individual journey each was about to undertake as they entered the Temple.

And that felt odd. All the very human insecurities raised their head as I had read this point.. me, as Great Mother? How… what could I, just me, bring to this? And that question, I realised, was also the answer. I could bring my Self, it is all we can ever do.

The costume was simple and symbolic, grey veiled in clouds of night, a girdle of stars, dark tears at my throat and a simple nine pointed circlet, beautifully crafted by Katie. All chosen for their simplicity and symbolism… especially the veil which prevented the pilgrims from seeing Her face, yet allowed them into her embrace. I thought I had it sorted.

I do not know and cannot tell what others felt. Only what I saw and felt myself. I stood in the silence of the sacred space and waited for the first of the companions to enter, a silent prayer in my heart, not knowing really what to do, simply trusting that I would know when the moment came. The bells called the companions in, and the first saluted the central Light and turned to me.

And it was simple. I just held out my arms and embraced them and the cloudy veil held them like dark wings.

It sounds very little. But, from my heart to yours, I tell you that this was the most profoundly moving thing. Each pair of eyes met mine with radiant joy, each heart was open and full of Light and Life and Love, each face lit with so much beauty. One after another I held them. Overwhelmed and humble, with a glowing, incandescent sun, it seemed, blazing in my heart.

I sat in silence to watch the drama unfold and behind the veil the tears slid across my cheeks to meet my smile.

It was I who was blessed.

# *Tyger Lady*
## *Katie Belle*

As I left Wales for Derbyshire that sunny Friday morning and made my way through vast mountains and valleys, market towns, villages and dark forests, I had no particular expectations of what might be in store that weekend. Admittedly I was a bit apprehensive – I barely knew anyone, felt under-experienced and the Ritual Workbook had got me in something of a tizz. Whilst Steve had kindly reassured me, I was still like a 'rabbit in headlights' over some of the lines, moves and layouts but of course he was right – it all worked perfectly on the day. The drive was so beautiful – full of anticipation, sunshine, lambs, red kites, buzzards and rocky outcrops – all against a sprouting backdrop of the Lady's verdant spring gown. Oh – and blue, blue skies... I was scooting along, happy and free, 'life is good' I thought – 'life is bloody good'!

The Ritual workbook however had provided another concern – I was horrified to find that the role I had been given was that of a rather aggressive Circus owner with a penchant for capturing and training big wild cats – shudders! As something of a free spirit myself and an animal rights advocate, her attitude and some of her script had my toes curling! I felt I couldn't possibly represent this woman with any conviction. However as my 7 hour drive to Derbyshire progressed I found myself getting more and more assertive and dare I say it, more like her in some respects. As the weekend and story unfolded I began to take a less literal view of her occupation and began to see through the layers of symbolism and appreciate the relevance of her character. I eventually came to look upon this formidable lady and her big cats in quite a different light.

On arrival the first people to greet me were Jordis and Matt, I was a tad nervous and clumsily blurted out that I had brought a fur stole with a view to making my entrance 'in character' but felt I hadn't quite got the 'sphericals' to carry it off. However on sight of Sue and Steve, without thinking I immediately wrapped myself in the stole and cried 'Darlings – let's get this show on the road!' It seemed that the Tyger Lady was making an appearance whether I liked it (and her) or not… and at that point I most certainly didn't!

The weekend was packed full – and I mean packed, early starts, a full schedule and late nights made them rather long days (to confess, the late nights were in the pub, but hey they dragged me there – honest, it's all Matt and Kevin's fault!). So packed, in fact, that at the time I didn't quite notice such a bond was forming, but form it did, I started hugging people – a lot. And the laughter, oh my, did we laugh, I recall dissolving into a helpless pool of giggles on Friday night! Without realising, it seemed a spiritual family had reunited and for me at least, the beauty of that reunion was in its natural, persuasive stealth… this gathering felt so very familiar and comfortable right from the very start. And so to the Work.

As the story of the Pilgrims unfolded, so did our characters. I went to my room after each Ritual to write up some notes and sometimes lie on the bed for a few minutes (with that fur stole hanging nearby which, with no small amount of guilt, I own – but that's another story altogether) musing on this feisty, fearless lady I was portraying. In particular I thought about the polarity of character traits, and whilst her character here was challenging and aggressive, these traits do have an opposite, positive aspect. I realised that there have been times when it would have been wise for me to encompass them – to have been more self-assured, confident and independent. I have also since mused on the Circus connection, and apparently the word originates from the Greek 'Krikos' meaning 'circle', and an early Christian writer claimed that circus games originated with the goddess Circe in honour of her father Helios the Sun god. All rather interesting given that our 'performances' were at points around the Enneagram circle and the School's birth was at sunrise on Sun-day under the watchful Eye of Horus.

Without effort and perhaps even without realising, we became increasingly drawn into the unfolding story, the challenges and interplay between the Troubadours, Keepers, Child and Pilgrims. There were many poignant moments, a personal one was when the King said some kind words to the Tyger Lady and kissed her hand. This gesture had touched me when I read through the script beforehand, but I wasn't quite prepared for its effect within the Temple setting – frankly she melted, her spiky armour fell away and there she was – vulnerable but not weak, exposed but not defenceless – his gentleness and kindness had dissolved her ego defences and restored her trust in her true self, it really was quite beautiful.

On Sunday morning (after a whole 4 hours sleep, yes you know who's fault that was!) I made my way down the Temple at 4.45am for the Vigil. I was heartened to see so many of us there at that crazy hour given our long journeys to get there, lack of sleep, another long day ahead and more travelling after that. Yet there we were, calmly, gently and in Silence we waited at the Temple doors.

I was the last to enter and walking towards Sue, who was sitting almost statue-like in a beautiful gown and veil, I was struck by how serene she looked. Indeed the whole room resonated with a gold flecked, diffused light and I felt as if I was stepping into another dimension, it was so still and pure… a sanctuary. When the time was right, Sue led everyone in total silence out of the Temple and through the sleeping, misty village which felt somewhat like the outer expression of an inner landscape, that of being 'awake' whilst surrounded by those who still 'sleep'. The first light gently illuminated the undulating landscape but all was still grey, there wasn't quite enough light to see the colours and in this I saw yet another analogy of spiritual awakening. As we passed the village boundary stone, a lamb came toward us and bleated several times – no one broke the silence but many smiled or gasped, recognising the significance of this little soul's cries…. and another gift – a hawk flew overhead to complete the blessing.

As the sunrise grew closer and closer, Steve and Sue brought their School into being. Once we had all had passed through the gateway formed by them both (creating a wonderful piece of symbolism) we stood in silence, holding that moment, with only the sounds of the natural world about us. I felt so honoured to be part of it and on finding myself holding Dean's hand – whose role was that of the King – I instinctively returned his kiss in an expression of gratitude. Congratulations were offered, photos were taken and the Company meandered their way down the hill and through the village back to the Centre – no doubt with hot drinks and breakfast in mind! Benjamin and I loitered, arm in arm we watched the glowing sun peep over the hill and rise up, its weak orange light slowly creeping across the rolling Derbyshire hills, chasing away those grey shadows.

The last Ritual that Sunday morning was potent. The story came to its climax and emotions ran high. Sue's voice trembled as she delivered her last line and as she moved to stand next to Steve I felt a wave of intense emotion blast across the circle from them both – this was it – the final moments of the final ritual and the Silent Eye School of Consciousness was well and truly conscious in its own right.... a leap of faith and months of work, sacrifice and emotion were about to come to fruition. I'd managed to hold it together during Ali's final, very moving, performance but now tears pricked my eyes and I had to take some deep breaths to compose myself as I prepared to take my leave of the Temple. Once we were all gathered outside in the hallway and the Temple doors were closed behind us for the last time, there was a tangible energy of completion and release.

At last, the School was alive and its energies were now afoot!

With thanks to Steve, Sue and my Companions of that weekend for their gifts – of privately spoken supportive words, shared stories and knowledge, kindness, hugs, laughter and tears. Such fond memories, I treasure each and every one. And my, what a fine gathering of human, hobbit, elf and faery folk we made!

Katie / | \

ps. I was partaking of a cup of tea as I tweaked the final draft and just noticed what was on my mug, sometimes we need to be Tyger – sometimes Tigger. The trick of course, is knowing when to be which.

# *The Fugitive's Tale*
## *Allan Pringle*

The "old places" still shine in the Derbyshire landscape. Driving through deep, cave-strewn gorges and up on to the high-land was a breathtaking introduction to the weekend. Great Hucklow, nestled within its distinct triangle of ritual mounds, could hardly have been a more perfect setting for what was about to unfold: the coming together of like minds and hearts to inhabit, witness and empower a singular moment of grace and beauty.

We walked in to, "… gonorrific seepage." Having obviously missed the health and safety briefing, we introduced ourselves to the assembled pilgrims, upholders, keepers and a surprisingly relaxed troubadour. By the time twenty-two disparate individuals sat down to break bread that evening, the group had already found its form: loving communion.

Entering temple for the first time can be an incredibly emotional experience. The concept of breaking in a ritual virgin gently is obviously absent from the teachings of the school, and it was a very nervous Osiris (type-cast to the end) who opened the play.

Two days then passed, in a flurry of dressing, undressing, feasting, drinking, raucous intercourse, moments of deeply moving intimacy, shared joy, deep, heartfelt laughter, tears… everything, in fact, that your average outsider imagines goes on at such events: only infinitely more powerful than they could hope to conceive, as hearts and minds bond and intertwine in a shared experience beyond words.

Coming from the "energy work" side, temple time was a revelation. The faltering vortex established in the first ritual, built, with the confidence of the players, to a pillar of pure light, shining, beacon-like, across the Derbyshire landscape, infusing the planetary grid, and beyond, with a statement of love and intent.

The lessons of the weekend are impossible to summarise. Though, for me, a high point occurred as the Child walked the pattern for the first time, raising a veil, such that, suddenly, the mire of the enneagram made sense! Though the mystery of eternity, the contraceptive properties of curried Brussel sprouts, and why reference to Bob Holness may reveal too much… will probably remain long after the initial clarity on the symbol has faded.

The culmination (almost), in the wee small hours of Sunday morning, was breathtaking in its simplicity and beauty. The night before, I was "given" the form of offering. Walking in to sacred space to find the layout altered from that expected, to exactly mirror both forms which I was about to present was more than a little shocking. In that moment, the insignificance of our individual "ego" interpretations of events, and, indeed, how ridiculous our "ego" fears of exposing oneself, completely, in the magical sense, really is; whether in the relative "safety" of group, or in the wider world at large.

And that's where they dumped us, unceremoniously, on Sunday afternoon – back into the wider world; there to assimilate the lessons of the weekend. I think all of us have, at some point in the days since, longed for a few more hours basking in the glow of joy, love and respect shared by the Companions of the Birthing.

# The Pilgrim and the Lamb
## Kevin Patrick

Oh to be a pilgrim!
"He who would Valiant be"
Hum or sing it as you feel fit. I bet by the day's end though you will to. The tune is hardwired in my brain still, as it plays its loop yet again, a remnant from earlier carefree days at school. Triggered, as experiences and memories of a rather unusual weekend unravel in my tired mind.
It's a catchy little number and bound to grab your attention, as many such songs have had a wont to do over the ages. The harmonies of the universe manifesting into the creation we have been dropped into. That's what some troubadours whom I recently met would have you believe.
Suffice to say I was changed by my experiences at the time, and also in ways yet to come, if events of the weekend were anything to go by.
They had a tale to tell those troubadours, one, which makes the Canterbury Tales look like a stroll in the park. A tale by any standards which was only matched in vibrancy and audacity by the colours of their robes, but even that paled into insignificance compared with the Glories of the One at the dawning of creation.
To be fair in the end the troubadours gave us a glimpse of what it was like, that dawning. It was like coming home and much more.
They say life's a beach – and then you fry!
The Song of the Troubadour was a bit like that, at least it 'felt' like that in the beginning. Ask some of those nine pilgrims, many of whom thought they had life sorted. Were they in for a shock, I mean –'shut up' – as some of our younger brethren would say these days.
Brought to sanctuary at the doorway of a monastery High in the mountains of Andasola, having suffered at the hands of a severe storm. Then fed and watered they slept waited for the storm to abate and continue on their journey.
Surprise!

To be woken in a strange Temple with a geometric design upon the floor. I mean freaky or what. But I digress and the tale is long in the telling. So let me explain, or at least give you a flavour of the shenanigans going on between the pilgrims at the start of their journey.

You see, the Troubadours were to blame; it was their fault that I found myself in this predicament. Dressed in threadbare robes with a belt the colour of the morning sun. Seated in some far-flung land called Andasola awaiting the first 'Knowledge Lecture'. With a draft of cold air ascending to my nether regions at the time, and cooling said parts, of which I will not describe in detail, for fear of upsetting the squeamish. I tell you, I was I glad that I was appointed a keeper of the Flame and able to use some of my abilities to add some warmth to the proceedings.

It was then that pattern, the 'Enneagram', which the pilgrims were to discover later on the floor of the temple made its first appearance.

Well the enneagram upon first impression looks a bit like some Klingon war bird or some sort of evolutionary successor to a Borg Cube. Or worse still my mind cried at the time, it might be some business model for corporate personality development. Images of purple ties and shirts, and women 'Power dressing' ran past my mind's eye aghast in horror, oh no!

But nothing could have been further from or closer to the truth as they say after another fashion. Who would have of thought that, in the middle of the Derbyshire countryside. Not since the adventures of Sean the sheep had I been so shaken. I mean I might have been getting fleeced and not recognised it. But I guess trust was the byword and I stuck to my guns, and kept an open mind. I was glad I did that.

Simply put dear reader what was going on was started by the appearance of a crazy looking diagram on a screen. Emblazoning itself upon my retina and pronouncing persona development and proclaiming links with my real self. A buzz in my crown chakra announcing it's okay, whilst the reverberations of a Shamanic drummer (Censer of sound) still beat a tattoo upon my consciousness from a previous session (by the way that Lad has got the tune of the universe in his head, if you know what I mean).

Yeh…as my thoughts meandered to an artist who had only just recently become an acquaintance, But whom I've known apparently for a Lifetime – at least my soul says, whatever that is – and who's to argue. Then into the mix some hot blond (a lady circus owner) with more understanding of the universe than she realises and a wonderful soul to boot, opens a conversation and I'm gob smacked.

"Which type are you" she says. Well you can imagine the thoughts rolling through my mind at the time, but I remained steadfast and meekly said "what do you mean?" Before I had time to reply (thank God) I was brought rapidly back to earth when the raised eyebrows of a nearby physician caught my attention.. Of course that conversation opened a whole can of worms….

A glance from a troubadour came in my direction – oops silence has its moments it seemed.

Then there was this precocious kid, the kind who tells you what you're really like, and whom you would like to give a clip behind the ear at some stage because they are so right (you just don't want admit it to yourself) – the innocence.

Those troubadours must have known something we didn't it, 'cos they called him The Child. I mean who calls an adult 'The Child'

And that dear readers was the start of the journey, of course there were more of those pilgrims, nine all told, characters of great remark who all had apart to play in the great adventure which was yet to unfold.

Funny though. Those pilgrims seemed to match the nine points on that Enneagram 'thingy'.

I need to have a word with those pesky Troubadours, they seem to have an idea as to what's going on. Oh and yes they could sing!

Blessings to you all

## *The Lamb*

I am a Lamb, at least,
That is what I am told those strange creatures –humans- know us by.
But today was a special day, I could tell!

The first hints of dawn were calling me to graze.
- As the Creator Wills -
But I snuggled close still to my mum.
The dew was still upon the grass of the fields.
As diamond points of creation upon the Land.
But a sudden impulse caused me to rise.
I'm glad I did.
As, a strange company floated by.

Strange that is – as seen by most human eyes.
Leading their company, were those dressed in the bright colours of the 'One'.
And behind, were other bright souls, a flock, ready to dance and greet him.
Just like when this world was first created.

My heart leapt with joy, they understood!
Shaking off the remnants of my sleep
I rushed forward.

Look, Look, I shouted!
He comes.

As the Hawk of the Morning flew overhead.
The Flame of the 'One' blazed into Life.
A New Day had begun.

I laughed and shouted with Joy

As the rays of His Love and Light fell upon us all.
-'Us' Lambs – you know we have been so Blessed.
We have been at the beginning of things, at many a time.
And will be for all Eternity.
So my mum says.
It was good to see you there.
So the next time you see me.
Please – Say Hello!

*Dedicated to those who were at the Birth of The Silent Eye.*
*With Much Love. Kevin*

# The Physician's Tale
## *Jordis Fasheh*

The closest way to describe our weekend together would be to say that we came together to embark upon the road with heart in the Hills and Dales of an ancient land and to discover our soul's oneness with all that is. A thousand individual rays of a prism refracted as the light of Christ coming together in sacred space to become conscious of who we are in perfection. As pilgrims and companions we travelled from distant places, a sojourn of a lifetime, to meet up in this magical place to light the torch and way home to the eternal one that I Am.

On day one, as my pilgrim's character, the Proud Physician, I brought with me a feeble attempt at intellectual pursuit and reach for knowledge in all the worldly sense of a healer. I meant to share what I had been studying before the weekend in attempt to prepare for our journey. However, sitting with Steve, Sue, Stuart, Dominique and Benjamin, I realized that our aim was one that would fulfil being. It was to go far beyond the intellect and into the realm of heart to connect with the infinite source of love and light. Of course, with Steve saying that there was no need to have the intellect in high gear, and that we are here to experience truth, I immediately shed the physicians cloak and opened up to what the weekend's journey through ritual and knowledge lectures had to offer. I felt welcome and held gently inside a warm and loving container.

We set off Friday evening, high in the mountains and crags of Andasola, the Gods, Keepers, and Powers, guided the Troubadours, child, and pilgrims out of the cold and turbulent storm that the dark shadows of our small selves created, into the present perfection of oneness with our highest Self. As the weekend and rituals unfolded, in light and love, as companions, we laughed and cried together from the core of our hearts. With Sue as the Great Mother, I reconnected with the eternal feminine and melted into the enfoldment of the wings of Isis. With Steve as progenitor, I felt safe and nurtured through his gentle nature, passionate vision and open heart. With Stuart, as the child and guiding light, along with the great King and Queen, through their own transformation and letting go, I was given to the moment of awakening, when in true form, I reconnected with source and saw my Higher Self and that of all of the companions, in the present perfection of being. And in glorious form on Sunday, early morning at dawn, blessed by the presence and joy of the singing lamb to welcome us into the fold and to help birth the school of the Silent Eye, we danced in the light of the Sun. Although, I wanted to run and shout, laugh and cry through the gateway that Sue and Steve held as High Priest and Priestess, I restrained myself and was the first to walk through, to proclaim that I have risen and declare my intention to join the new school.

Truly, I laughed and cried with a fine bunch of folk from diverse backgrounds who brought with them acceptance for all, angels and demons alike. We stayed up until the wee hours of the night talking, sharing and listening to one another. The greatest gift of the weekend was the restoration of my inner sight and the reopening of my heart centre, awakening to the glorious beauty of who we are as divine emanations in this vast and splendid world.

Thank you to Sue and Steve for the remarkable journey through ritual and the opportunity to walk through a new doorway and for consciousness to know itself as creation's perfection. Thank you to Stuart for your soft and gentle guidance as the child of light. Thank you to all of the upholders; Matt who brings the creative fire to his fabulous photography, to Benjamin a brilliant painter and sound technician, Adam a sacred drummer and everyone who spent time and energy building the temple and creating and holding sacred space. Thank you to the companions who made me laugh until my belly ached and warming my heart with your authentic and charming selves. And Alienora for scaring the life out me during the dancer's last attempt at wielding enough power to save the pilgrims. To Dean for your marvellous tales of survival and conquering the wild forces of nature including sea crocs, tiger sharks, the hundred eyes of alligators in the

Everglades, accidentally treading upon a giant black mamba and then running for your life, unknowingly sleeping next to tarantulas and black widows, and saving a hare's life while providing it shelter and safety from the hounds and their masters. To Kevin for your bawdy sense of humour. And of course, to Matt for your incredible ability of transforming the serious and severe into light hearted and funny stories. Especially enjoyed the story of putting up with al dente Brussel sprouts smothered in a full bottle of cold Coleman's Curry as the main and only course while listening to a complaint about Irritable Bowel Syndrome! And to Katie for your kind sensibilities, and bold humour, especially after scaring off the woman at the Pub! And really everyone for all of your stories, wisdom, counsel and most of all your generosity of heart. While I am from San Francisco, I left my heart with all of you in Great Hucklow. Cheers to all and until we meet again, in love and light!

# *The Artist's Eye*
## *Sue Vincent*

Looking around the assembled faces as we sat waiting to begin the first of the lectures on the Saturday morning, it occurred to me how many artists of all types were sitting there.
From the professional to the gifted in visual arts, the musicians and the dancers, the writers and poets, our consummately talented photographer, a maker of beautiful things and the creative gifts of the Temple team…it was quite astonishing.

*Steve, brush in hand*

I cannot wait to share some more of the photographs created by Matt that show how a simple room can be transformed into a sacred space. I have seen only the unedited shots and they are spectacular. And there is one shot that will, I think, capture the essence of the weekend in the most amazing fashion. But we all have to wait for the work to be done on that image.
There were drums. The most beautiful and profound of music, both visceral and haunting in the temple as Adam used sound in place of incense to symbolically bless and purify the working space. His is a rare

gift and those moments when he and the drum seemed to become one, both with each other and with something beyond both, will, I think, live in our hearts and memories a very long time.

There was music. Alienora with fiddle, recorder and piano, joining Adam in the library and filling it with laughter and sound.

There was Steve, the Troubadour, guitar in hand, seated in the Temple as he and I sang the song we had written for the School.

There was the painting created by all. Disjointed impressions, symbols and words that somehow came together to create an energy on canvas that captured the bright spirit of the companions and the time out of time that we shared. Matt's otherworldly artistic impression of what was created shows, I think, the soul of what was placed on that canvas. And an email from Kevin that reduced me to tears placed Ani's paw print among the symbols as, he wrote, "she must be an honorary Nerk 1st Degree by now at least. A trace of her soul should be on it I think, she has journeyed with you all the way."

There was the cake, decorated with the symbol of the Silent Eye by our wonderful Lil, shared before the companions departed on the Sunday.

There were three small paintings from Benjamin, gifted to me before he left me yesterday, that capture the depth and beauty of what was wrought over those few days and how it touches the life and heart of those who take that leap of faith into the inner landscape.

And there were words. Humour, banter and wilful misinterpretation causing riotous, and as Alienora describes in her post, of raucous laughter. Small things said in quiet moments that leave an indelible impression on the heart. Words written and spoken in beauty and the overwhelming sense of loving kinship that was shared as we were bound together in our journey. Words unspoken, poems crafted by the heart and written in eyes that met, sharing smiles and love in a place and a moment outside of time.

# *A Magical Birth*
## *Sue Vincent*

There are some things for which words are never enough. Things it is almost impossible to share. There are some things which should not be shared, perhaps, but the birth of the School was symbolic and not just for those who could be with us on that Derbyshire dawn.

So here I will share how it was through my eyes, holding nothing back, for it was never mine to keep, only to live.

This telling will be longer than usual, and yet will only skim the surface of that morning. I offer it from my heart to all those who could not be with us on the hillside on Sunday morning. There were many who were with us in thought and prayer across the world, some who shared with us the weekend yet who could not physically make the climb up the hill. These people, many of whom have been with us every step of the way, who have shared our laughter and tears, have taught so much through their loving support. I offer this telling to those who guided our steps over the years, who held our hands and opened our minds.

We carried you in our hearts. Now see through my eyes.

"...*They* have always been ready, now you must bring it to birth..."

At 3.20 in the morning I stood outside the centre in my dressing gown under a canopy of deepest velvet blue sprinkled with stars. The sky was clear and mild, lacking the biting frost that had glittered under the previous dawn.

There was no nervousness, just a deep serenity, a knowing and a purpose in the silence.

I breathed deeply, filling myself with the clear air and night's beauty. Already tears pricked my eyelids, knowing what was to come to birth. Months of constant work, lifetimes of preparation for both of us. The culmination of an incubation nurtured in silence. The birth of a dream.

I closed my eyes and offered a silent prayer, asking the blessing of the One on what we were about to do, quietly reaching out across a sleeping world to touch in thought and love all those who had brought us to this moment, and to the little mother, so far away, whom I have loved so very much for so long. She too is part of this as we carry forward a spark of the Light she showed us.

There was a sadness too, a gentle sadness, as I saw a familiar life slip away and prepared to step onto a new path that will carry me where it must. Though I go willingly and without regret, there is always a sadness when the current lifts you away from the life and love of the past. Though the outer life may seem little different, the inner one also came to birth that morning.

As I showered and robed I could feel love around me, the fleeting caress of other minds and hearts, as if those who watched around the world left butterfly kisses on my brow. I was not alone in my solitary room. The sense of presence was tangible and warm. Following a dream a few nights before I dressed in the gold of dawn with jewels like gilded dew at my throat. I remember looking back at the room, strewn with robes and colour, wondering.

I knocked on Steve's door to leave my key. He opened it, robed in blue, the Eye of Horus on his breast, golden. In silence he bowed and I walked alone to the temple.

The lights were low, I took my place in the centre of the ancient symbol, hallowed by the hearts and minds of the companions. At my feet the golden chalice, engraved with the symbol of the sun, holding only light. I composed myself and the vigil began.

For a while there were the fleeting thoughts as the mind settled into stillness. Who would come at this unearthly hour? After a night of conviviality in pub and library, little sleep and with long journeys ahead later in the day? A few, I hoped. Few I expected. It was an unfair thing to ask. Yet it was symbolic, it mattered only that we were there and played out in the waking world what we had been given to do.

With my eyes half closed the golden light from the chalice seemed to fill the room. The temple itself was a chalice, itself not important, only its function, to give shape and hold what was pouring into it. At the centre I saw myself, still, golden, unfamiliar. I too was only a cup, a container to hold and shape that fluid Light we serve. Around me, spiralling like leaves in an autumn wind, it seemed as if motes of brightness danced with the shadows and the sparkling expectancy was palpable, like the air before a storm. I felt a strong sense of presence. Myself, sitting motionless on the chair, others, unseen, arcing around that tiny point of light in the centre. Holding vigil in the silence with the Mother.

The door opened and he who walked that morning in the robe of the Father came in and sat before me. The eyes that met seemed not our own, the hands that met in blessing and greeting felt other than our own. He broke the silence, but the few words spoken were not simply his own and had their place in that moment.

He took his place on my right, his left hand outstretched resting on my shoulder and the vigil continued. Like another note added to a song in harmony, the feel of the room changed and took on depth and the sense of presence became more profound. Some time later the Child entered. He too sat before me, with eyes I shall not forget, glowing with love in that moment. A gesture, an offering that brought serene tears to my eyes. They were not my hands. Then he too took up his place on my left, his right hand on my shoulder, and the harmony deepened.

Shapes touched the edge of vision, whispers of song in the silence, words unspoken that I will seek for a lifetime. I felt caught between worlds in a vast, womblike cavern as an unseen heart beat beneath my feet. Unfamiliar even to myself.

I saw shadows through the tiny window of the door, others were there. The silence was absolute, their gift to the moment. Then the door was opened and the companions filed in, one by one, to take their place before the Mother and silently offer, heart to heart, and receive what was offered in stillness.

And they were all there. All those who could be there, all who could walk up that pre-dawn hillside. All of them.

I cannot describe the feeling in that moment, the outpouring of loving blessing, the gifts given by people who should have been asleep for hours to come, yet who had sacrificed their rest and joined us in silent vigil. The eyes that met mine as I watched through the lens of tears at the beauty before me. Through the other eyes, it seemed, lent to me for a moment out of time. The hearts that were open, the smiles, all gentle, the one who knelt and gave all he was to that moment and the unknown moments to come.

They took their places around the circle, forming what felt like great wings holding the Light within. I closed my eyes and gathered the threads of Light in my heart.

At the appointed time I rose, placed a cloak around my shoulders and led them from the room, pausing to allow them to don their coats, the silence incredible in the soft light.

The morning was mild and beautiful, the sky streaked with colour, the rose and blue, the hint of gold, painted by the Master Hand. We walked slowly through the sleeping village, silent ghosts in strange garb climbing the hill to the gate.

Yet there was no strangeness, only a sense of rightness in the moment…present and not present, watching within and without, and the utter silence. Beyond the low wall to the right a young lamb looked up, bleating, eye to eye, three times. As if we were being given a blessing, recognition, acknowledgement. Such a simple thing, but so very beautiful.

We walked up the dew damp slope, to the little lawn between the tree to the west and the notch in the bare fingered trees in the east, silhouetted against the growing light. We placed the chalice and plate on the altar and Father and Mother stood to greet the dawn.

Those moments of waiting, in the miraculous silence made only deeper by the symphony the birds were singing, are some that will live in my heart forever. The small arc of the companions felt like a great host behind us as we raised our arms to salute the sun in its rising, and the greater Light it symbolises.

Turning to each other, arms still raised, we became the gate of dawn, a portal through which the Child could pass. Our arms extended, eyes holding, unable to see beyond the raised arms, we saw the Child come within our embrace and pass through to the Light as we broke the silence with a single chanted word. *Cromaat*.

The weight of the cloak against my throat was too much, I let it fall. Overhead a hawk wheeled in the dawn glow.

One by one the companions passed through the gate that we were, emerging on the other side to be greeted by the Child. They were asked why they had passed through the gates of Light and Life… to the Child who is Love. In turn, they answered, the first giving the response of those who have chosen to walk with us in the School, these were anointed with consecrated oil and accepted. Those who were with us in love and support affirmed the wholeness of the One. Together they formed the wings of morning before the gate.

When all had passed into the east, we proclaimed the birth of the Silent Eye and, blessing bread and wine, we broke our fast in shared communion on a hillside bathed in gold and birdsong.

With laughter, many embraces, very many tears and smiles, our School came to birth as the son rose and something new was brought into the world with joy and with Love.

# *A Kiss from the Sun*
## *Steve Tanham*

It was Sue who started it. As is her way, she, innocently (!) mentioned a few weeks ago that, try as I might, my years of working closely with Dolores Ashcroft-Nowicki, the Director of Studies of SOL, had made me into an effective and hard-core Magician. No matter what my protestations, Sue said, about the fact that there needed to be new ways and new Paths to embrace both science and the growing body of knowledge from Depth Psychology, I was and always would be a Magician.

Hmmm.

On Saturday night, in the heart of the Derbyshire Hills, surrounded by 22 tired but enthusiastic folk playing their hearts out in the third ritual drama of the day to achieve the potency in the room that the words on the page promised, I gave in to that sentiment, and decided that, for all my stubbornness, I would finally surrender to that notion and ensure that the Silent Eye combined the best of both those worlds.

Over the seven years that we worked together, there were many beautiful gifts from Dolores; but the greatest thing she taught me was not to be afraid of innovation, particularly when it came to Ritual Drama (for two Geminis with Scorpio rising you may not be surprised).

Far more that my Rosicrucian mentors before her, she showed, by example, what you can do with ritual in a relatively small space when the participants come together with a loving and integrity-filled purpose, to make true Magic, which is simply the raising of Consciousness; and the sheer force (read not-simply) of personal transformation that it brings. I think I probably graduated from her tutoring during the first of the preceding Alchemy workshops, also held at the Nightingale Centre, but this weekend we entered a new space, with a new agenda under the solar wings of the Silent Eye School.

In that now-hallowed memory in time and place, we manifested a real a group of pilgrims lost in the mountains in a ferocious storm, and rescued by the presence of a mystic monastery where the Keepers wove a magical journey of psychological discovery from the raw material of nine strong characters and the catalyst of two troubadours plus young man whose negative Ego had never developed, leaving him free to see the world and its distorted inhabitants for what they are . . . and could be.

As a teacher of such things, I cannot think of a more effective way to contribute to the minds and hearts of those who will enter our new School, or the traditions from which I journeyed.

And after this wonderful weekend, I wouldn't want to.

So bring on the sweet-smelling new Earth, the singing Lamb dancing by the stream along the way, the beautiful Sunrise in a soft blue sky and above all, the company of wonderful and sincere Souls who put their inner development high in importance in their lives.

A Kiss from the Sun, indeed.

# *The School*

The Silent Eye School offers a spiritual journey into yourself and the meaning of your own life.

It is aimed at people who have reached what we call the "turning point" in their lives. Young or not so young, they feel, with a growing inner conviction, that the things of the world no longer provide real nourishment; and that, somewhere along the stream of their lives, they lost a deeper sense of reality.

Not even family and friends can make a difference to this feeling, which is deeply personal. This state, which is actually a very positive one, is the call of our own deeper selves. We say this in the context of attention to self, not in the sense of selfishness. The two are very different things.

We offer a modern and dynamic distance-learning programme, with personal supervision. We are a not-for-profit organisation and only seek to cover our costs.

**"Who am I?"**

It's a question we should ask ourselves every day.

The scientific view is that you are human animal, driven by biological needs. Over and above these, you insert personal and possibly spiritual values to give more meaning to your life.

Psychology and, if you are fond of it, astrology, tell you that you also have a unique personality, made up of some planetary influences at birth, and modified by the experiences in your life. Either way, you have ended up a very complex thinking/feeling/surviving individual.

So why do we feel estranged from that deep sense of another, deeper, reality?

The Silent Eye programme offers you a chance to explore this question and to launch a very structured, and often humorous, investigation into you . . .

## Join us on a journey

Well, three journeys, to be precise; one taken each year for three years.
The first journey is to investigate something that psychology calls your "Ego". It's your personality, really, or at least the conscious bits of it, the everyday characteristics with which you manage, and react to, your life. But it's also the outer shell of your whole being.
Rather than instruct you with a formal, textbook approach, we take you on a journey of the mind, based on techniques learned in the world of magical pathworking and ritual drama. This animates the inner exploration and involves the whole being – intellect, emotions and the edge of spirituality.
It's a challenging mixture of levity and very serious study. You might like it . . .
The journey – your journey, begins in a desert, where you will meet a wonderful, if slightly enigmatic Guide...
Building on the wisdom of some of the best modern practitioners of esoteric psychology, we integrate the use of the enneagram as a map of the self's return – a quest to find in our personalities the keys to our inner hunger for reality, and the starting points of that voyage of self-discovery.
You are not what you take yourself to be. Your personality is built from reactions to the world, reactions over which you had no control. But you do have control of what happens now in your life.

## The Land of the Exiles

A landscape brought to life, explored and then revealed for what it is.
A desert journey where you don't know the rules, but have to follow the kindly but challenging guide, who watches your progress at every step, well, most of the time, anyway.
A journey begun in passivity, where strange figures are encountered, who then begin to reveal their inner natures, all the time showing you yours .

The Land of the Exiles: a Kingdom without a King and Queen, or is it? The start of your journey begins here. But it will take you farther than you can know . . .

A reclusive and cloaked figure in a tall tower who knows the Land of the Exiles very well, but needs to stay isolated from it; An Angry Queen in Winter; a Celebrated Actor of tragedies who holds crowds spellbound in the thrall of his melancholy tales. These are but a few of the women and men you will meet on the journey through the first degree of the Silent Eye's distance learning programme.

At the end of this first year, you will know the structure of your personality very well, but, more fundamentally, you will know the signposts that show you the way home, unique to each of us and written in our character.

To stand on the edge of the world of Being, is to see that our lives to date have been lived, literally, in the shadows.

The first year's journey around the outer shell of our own self is a challenging journey to make, for we must meet and face the truth about ourselves, without which spiritual progress is impossible.

The Silent Eye School of Consciousness is a modern Mystery School that seeks to allow its students to find the inherent magic in living and being. With students around the world the School offers a fully supervised and practical correspondence course that explores the Self through guided inner journeys and daily exercises. It also offers workshops in a variety of forms and locations that combine sacred drama, lectures and informal gatherings to bring the teachings to life in a vivid and exciting format. Full details of the School and all future events may be found on the official website, where there is also a forum open to all: **www.thesilenteye.co.uk**

*About the author:* Steve is a well-known figure in the esoteric world and has been a keynote presenter at many conferences and workshops. Born into a Rosicrucian family in Bolton, Lancashire, in 1954, Steve grew up surrounded by mystical discussion and fascinating but often peculiar grown-ups.

In adult life, and alongside a career in IT, he became an officer and then the Lodge Master of AMORC's John Dalton Chapter in Manchester. After having a decade off to help raise their two boys through the early stage of their lives, he returned to active mystical service and was soon asked to take a field officer role with the Rosicrucian Order, AMORC. This began an intensive seven year period of service culminating in the role of Grand Councilor for the North of England, Scotland and Ireland.

Steve retired from AMORC in 2005 with full military honours and fond memories of some wonderful times shared, including a final initiation in the King's Chamber of the Great Pyramid of Gizeh - something not easily bettered!

Shortly after, he met Dolores Ashcroft-Nowicki, Director of Studies of the Servants of the Light School, and her husband Michael, then in charge of all the back-office systems for SOL. It was a prophetic meeting as Steve was, shortly thereafter, to create SOL's computerised administration systems for Dolores and Michael, set up a SOL Lodge in Manchester, and become a founding member of the ARC Administration team to establish SOL's online presence and offer the lessons to a world-wide audience via the internet and electronic payment systems. Part of this undertaking was to be invited into SOL's House of the Amethyst and take the SOL highest initiation - the Third Degree - Adept.

Steve writes a personal blog at: lakesteve.blogspot.co.uk

# Other Books by Silent Eye Authors....

## LAND OF THE EXILES

A Silent Eye Workbook with Practical Notes

By Steve Tanham

*With contributions from Sue Vincent, Stuart France and the Companions of the Hawk.*

In April 2014 the Silent Eye, a modern Mystery School, hosted the Land of the Exiles as a weekend workshop. These annual gatherings attract people from across the world to share a unique approach to the spiritual journey that is taken by all. Over the course of the workshop a story unfolds, dramatic and emotive, engaging the hearts and minds of the participants, shadowing forth the challenges of the inner journey to awakening. This workbook includes the script from that journey, along with practical and explanatory notes, as well as the personal accounts of some of the Companions who shared an epic journey of the imagination as a spaceship crash-lands on a far-flung planet, and a cyborg forces them to play out the story of the ancient gods of Egypt, intent of calculating just what it means to be human…

A practical guide to a fully scripted ritual workshop from the Silent Eye, a modern Mystery School.

Illustrated

# THE INITIATE:

## Adventures in Sacred Chromatography

## Sue Vincent & Stuart France

### Foreword by Steve Tanham

Imagine wandering through an ancient landscape wrought in earth and stone, exploring the sacred sites of peoples long ago and far away in time and history. The mounds and barrows whisper legends of heroes and magic, painted walls sing of saints and miracles and vision seeps through the cracks of consciousness.

Now imagine that the lens of the camera captures a magical light in soft blues and misty greens and gold. A light that seems to have no cause in physical reality. What would you do?

If you were open to the possibility of deeper realities, perhaps you would wish to explore this strange phenomenon...something two people came to know as sacred chromatography.

The Initiate is the story of just such a journey beyond the realms of our accustomed normality. It is a factual tale told in a fictional manner. In this way did the Bards of old hide in the legends and deeds of heroes those deeper truths for those who had eyes to see and ears to hear.

As the veils thin and waver, time shifts and the present is peopled with the shadowy figures of the past, weaving their tales through a quest for understanding and opening wide the doors of perception for those who seek to see beyond the surface of reality.

Over 60 Full Colour Illustrations

# THE HEART OF ALBION:

### Tales from the Wondrous Head

### Stuart France & Sue Vincent

"If I am consciously following a woman who is about to engage a Llama in conversation, which I certainly appear to be, it does not impinge too negatively upon my thought processes."

What does Jack and the Beanstalk have to do with a spiritual quest? What, for that matter, is the nature of the relationship between Salome and the Jester? Why is Wen conversing with a llama in the Yorkshire Dales? And what links the beautiful and sacred landscape that is the Heart of Albion with Breakfast in Slug Town? These, and many other questions, must be considered as Don and Wen continue the journey begun in The Initiate exploring the shadowy roots of the ancient myths and legends of these Blessed Isles, steering a perilous path through the murky waters of religious symbolism and iconography.

"Breakfast in Slug Town?"

Join them on their continuing quest for knowledge and understanding as they explore the landscape of England and people it with strange creatures and even stranger theories, using sacred intent and guided imagination to penetrate into the mysteries unfolding before them.

Illustrated in full colour throughout

# SWORD OF DESTINY

## Sue Vincent

"...and the swords must be found and held by their bearers lest the darkness find a way into the heart of man. Ask the waters to grant guidance and tell the ancient Keeper of Light that it is time to join battle for the next age."

Rhea Marchant heads north to the wild and beautiful landscapes of the Yorkshire Dales where she is plunged into an adventure that will span the worlds. The earth beneath her feet reveals its hidden life as she and her companions are guided by the ancient Keeper of Light in search of artefacts of arcane power. With the aid of the Old Ones and the merry immortal Heilyn, the company seek the elemental weapons that will help restore hope to an unbalanced world at the dawn of a new era.

" Sue writes with a real grasp of the human side of people which is expressed in the personalities of her heroes and the recognizable characters that they interact with. The power and essence of her story is found in the admixture of her undoubted love of Yorkshire, her ability to see the warm and the good in all people, and her knowledge of the magical forces one can find at work in such places and between such folk. An inspired piece of writing that keeps your attention until the very last page."

*Dr G.M.Vasey, author of "The Last Observer" and "Inner Journeys: Explorations of the Soul ", co-author of "The Mystical Hexagram: The Seven Inner Stars of Power".*

# THE LIVING ONE:

## Contemplations on the Gospel of Thomas

### Stuart France

"...It is like the smallest of seeds and if it falls on prepared soil, it produces the largest of plants and shelters the birds of heaven..."

Many scholars believe that the Gospel According to Thomas preserves a glimpse into the oral traditions of the Gospels. The book is a collection of sayings, parables and dialogues attributed to Jesus and forms part of the Nag Hammadi Library, a collection of ancient papyri found near the Dead Sea in 1945.

In this unique interpretation Stuart France brings the oral tradition to life, retelling the Gospel in his own words, in the way it may have been shared around the hearthfires of our forefathers. Deeply entwined with the story is the personal journey to understanding, following it down some rather unusual pathways. It begins with a road trip in an arid landscape far from home; a journey that led through a country that captured imagination and set it to music. It ends with an ancient story, told as you have never read it before.

**"Look, it's obvious, mozzies are God's Angels in disguise."**

Accompanied by a commentary which draws upon the esoteric traditions of the Mystery Schools, The Living One provides a new window on an age old story, being a transmutation of the spirit of the words, born of the personal realisations of a seeker after Truth.

> **"Salome said to Joshua, "Who are you mister, you have eaten from my table and climbed on to my couch as if you are a stranger ?""**

# THE MYSTICAL HEXAGRAM:

## The Seven Inner Stars of Power

### Dr G. Michael Vasey & S.C. Vincent

**Foreword by Dolores Ashcroft-Nowicki**

The Mystical Hexagram is a new book by Dr G. Michael Vasey and S.C. Vincent. The book explores a symbol. Not from some scholarly or deeply complex perspective, but seeing it as a representation relating to life and living. The forces and pressures that are associated with the hexagram are, after all the forces of life at both practical and Universal levels. By exploring and beginning to understand the symbol, we are able to learn and discover more about ourselves.

The meditations throughout the book take you on an inner journey of exploration, discovering the parallels between the self and the greater reality within which we live our lives. They illustrate the connection between the inner and outer world of the self and the cosmic forces of Creation. Having traced that connecting path, the meditations offer a practical way of applying that understanding.

In addition to the exercises the book includes two very special meditations, The Garden of Remembrance and the Circle of Healing. These two you will want to revisit many times, taking away from the experience a sense of peace and beauty.

# THE OSIRIAD
## Isis & Osiris, the Divine Lovers

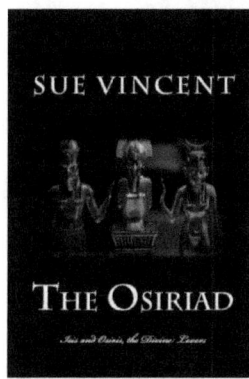

### Sue Vincent

"There was a time we did not walk the earth. A time when our nascent essence flowed, undifferentiated, in the Source of Being."

In forgotten ages, the stories tell, the gods lived and ruled amongst men. Many tales were told, across many times and cultures, following the themes common to all mankind. Stories were woven of love and loss, magic and mystery, life and death. One such story has survived from the most distant times. In the Two Lands of Ancient Egypt a mythical history has been preserved across millennia. It begins with the dawn of Creation itself and spans one of the greatest stories ever to capture the heart and imagination. Myths are, by their very nature, organic. They grow from a seed sown around a hearthfire, perhaps, and the stories travelled the ancient highways, embellished and adapted with each retelling. Who knows what the first story told?

In this retelling of the ancient story it is the Mistress of all Magic herself who tells the tale of the sacred family of Egypt.

"We have borne many names and many faces, my family and I. All races have called us after their own fashion and we live their stories for them, bringing to life the Universal Laws and Man's own innermost heart. We have laughed and loved, taught and suffered, sharing the emotions that give richness to life. But for now, I will share a chapter of my family's story. One that has survived intact through the millennia, known and remembered still, across your world. Carved in stone, written on papyrus, I will tell you of a time when my name was Isis."

# NOTES FROM A SMALL DOG:

## Four Legs on Two

## Sue Vincent

"He asked me what it is with balls…why I love them so much. I had a think about that. It is 'cause they fly. Like birds. I'm supposed to chase birds. I'm a bird-dog. 'Course, she won't really let me. It doesn't stop me barking at 'em and seeing 'em off from my garden. But it isn't the same. Somewhere, deep inside, I know what I am supposed to do, what I am supposed to be. But I can't be that for some reason… things aren't quite set up right for me to chase birds all day and bring them back to her. On the other hand, that's who I am…and you can't be anything else than that… so the balls let me be myself in a world where I can't catch birds all day.

She says that's not unusual… She seems to think that we all know who we really are, deep down, and that we spend all our time trying to find a way to be that in a world that doesn't quite seem to fit. We either find other stuff to express it…like balls…. Or we try and be what others think we should be… But you can't be a terrier if you are a retriever, can you? A bit like asking a fish to climb trees. It can be done, but it isn't easy!"

Ani, a very familiar spirit, was named for one of the ancient gods. It should, I suppose, have been no surprise when she took over the keyboard and began to write. A year later she had me collect her writings into a single volume at the insistence of her fans... who have been taken by her playful love of life and her odd wisdom...largely because she is saving for an automatic tennis ball launcher. The book is a collection of Ani's periodic posts, Notes from a Small Dog, on scvincent.com, with some other pieces she has asked me to include. She even lets me write occasionally… By this time you may, of course, think I am barking mad myself… you may have a point… but I stand with Orhan Pamuk, "Dogs do speak, but only to those who know how to listen."

# DOOMSDAY: THE ÆTHELING THING

### Stuart France & Sue Vincent

*Book One of the Doomsday Triad*

*"Who was this Arviragus bloke anyway?"*

Don studies the light as it plays through his beer, casting prisms on the table. How is it possible to hide such a story... the hidden history of Christianity in Britain? Oh, there are legends of course... old tales... Yet what if there was truth in them? What was it that gave these blessed isles such a special place in the minds of our forefathers? There are some things you are not taught in Sunday School...

From the stone circles of Northern England to the legendary Isle of Avalon, Don and Wen follow the breadcrumbs of history and forgotten lore to uncover a secret veiled in plain sight.

Illustrated in Full Colour throughout.

**All books are available from Amazon worldwide,**

**in paperback and for Kindle.**

www.ingramcontent.com/pod-product-compliance
Lightning Source LLC
Chambersburg PA
CBHW071511040426
42444CB00008B/1594